TRIB SERIES VOL 1

SERMON ON THE MOUNT

THE BELIEVER'S HANDBOOK

REV DAVID R BROOM JR.

DEDICATION

I would like to dedicate this book to my mother, Angel Broom.
Who, when I was young, encouraged me and tirelessly worked with
me in the ministry. Whatever the Lord led me to do, she never
questioned and gladly submitted to the will of the Lord, though I
was but seventeen. That brief time I walked away from God, she
never ceased to pray for me. Thank you Mama for always being
there for me.

CONTENTS

PREFACE

As I was working on the TRIB™ New Testament, book of Matthew, most notably the "Sermon on the Mount", the Lord laid it upon my heart to write a book for those believers that are just starting out their journey with Him. And not only new believers, but believers who have been led to believe that once salvation is received, it is a free ride through the narrow gate with no commandments to keep.

The Apostle Paul, in two places in the New Testament, speaks of the law of Christ. (Galatians 6:2; 1 Corinthians 9:21) Many speculations have been given about what the law of Christ is, but it is my opinion that is the commandments that Christ gave believers in the Sermon on the Mount.

This serves as a field manual, if you will, for the new believer and the seasoned veteran who has served Christ for many years. It is written with the new believer in mind, using very few theological terms in the explanations. In fact, it is written in every day English. Well, at least every day English in the southern portion of the United States.

Millions of people will die and go to hell believing they were serving Christ. Jesus said, "If you love me, keep my commandments." And just what commandments was He talking about? I am certain He didn't tell us to keep His commandments and then forget to give them to us. No, He spent three chapters in Matthew laying out His commandments for believers to follow. Very few of us follow every one of them.

I believe after reading this book, you will pay more attention to what Jesus really expects from His followers. If we really live by what Christ expects of us, it is a constant battle to serve Him. He said the road is rough that leads to the narrow gate and few will actually find their way.

You will learn that simply believing in Christ is not enough, as Jesus' earthly brother, James, will very plainly point out, as will the Apostle John. While the Gentiles were never under the Law of Moses, we do have commandments that we must obey if we claim to be a Christian. I pray you find this book to be a blessing and an eye opener, and I urge you to make sure every new believer you know reads this. If you can't afford to buy them a copy, let them read yours. I could care less about selling additional books, I just want to snatch every soul I possibly can out of the hands of Satan before he leads them down that broad road of destruction straight to hell.

Your Brother In Christ,

Rev. David R Broom Jr.

THE GOSPEL ACCORDING TO

SAINT MATTHEW

THE SERMON ON THE MOUNT

CHAPTER 5

¹ And seeing the large crowd, He went up into the mountain: and after He sat down, His disciples came to Him. ² And He opened His mouth and taught them, saying,

³ Blessed are the poor in spirit, for the kingdom of heaven is theirs.

Luke 6:20 simply states, "Blessed are the poor", excluding "in spirit". Was Jesus speaking to those who are humble ("poor in spirit") or was He speaking to those in poverty, or both?

Blessed simply means "happy". Why would those who are poor be happy? The bible says that riches produce anxiety, stress and the danger of not being able to enter into the kingdom of heaven. The poor do not have the temptations or stress that earthly riches bring. We can know that worldly riches alone do not bring happiness by looking at those, for instance, in Hollywood that seem to have it all and still commit suicide or end up on drugs just to cope with life.

What else does the bible say about the poor?

The gospel is preached to the poor, Luke 4:18; Matthew 11:5.

> "The blind regain their sight and the lame walk, the lepers are cleansed and the deaf regain their hearing, the dead are raised and the poor have the gospel preached to them." – Matthew 11:5

It was prophetically predicted that Jesus Himself would preach to the poor;

> "The Spirit of the Lord Yahweh is upon me, because Yahweh has anointed me to preach the gospel to the poor. He has sent me to heal the brokenhearted, to proclaim deliverance to the captives, and freedom to those in prison;" – Isaiah 61:1

It is easier for the poor to receive salvation, Matthew 19:23; Luke 18:24

> "And when Jesus saw that he became very sad, He said, how difficult it is for those who have worldly wealth to enter into the kingdom of God!" – Luke 18:24

Being a disciple of Jesus requires sacrifice, and it is hard for one who is rich too often to make the sacrifices required.

SERMON ON THE MOUNT: THE BELIEVER'S HANDBOOK

While it is not impossible for one who is rich to be saved, only those who are willing to give it all up when Jesus asks you to do so are spiritually mature enough to handle earthly wealth.

The humble and the poor are happy because they depend on Jesus, not worldly wealth. And for doing so, they shall inherit the kingdom of heaven. If you are blessed to have worldly wealth, pray for humility and an obedient spirit to Christ and you too will inherit the kingdom of heaven.

⁴ Blessed are those who grieve, for they shall be comforted.

> "For godly grief brings about repentance without regret: but the grief of the world produces death." – 2 Corinthians 7:10

There are several types of grief. Godly grief, where your heart is heavy and you are feeling grieved, either over a sin you have committed, or by the leading of the Holy Spirit that is tugging at your heart string and inviting you to have a relationship with Jesus. This is godly "good" grief. You will be comforted either by confessing your sins and repenting or by declaring that you believe in Jesus and asking Him to come live inside of you.

Then there is the emotional grief, the one that is brought on by losing a loved one, or a divorce, losing a job or the numerous other things that can cause us to grieve here in this world.

> "Take My yoke upon you and learn from Me, for I am gentle and humble inside, and you will find rest for your souls." – Matthew 11:29

A yoke is a wooden crosspiece that is fastened over the neck of two animals and then connected to a plow or some type of cart. It is made to distribute the load to both animals so one animal is not burdened down by the full load.

Jesus is simply saying, put your neck in the wooden crosspiece with me and let me carry your load. By letting Him carry our load, we find rest for our souls. By this, we are comforted when we grieve. If you have something that is really bothering or hurting you, give it to Jesus friend. You will find there is true comfort and peace in Jesus.

5 Blessed are the humble, for they shall inherit the earth.

What does it mean to be humble? It is having a low estimate of your own self-importance. For example, the Apostle Paul said:

> "To me, who is the very least of all saints, is this grace given, that I should preach among the Gentiles the fathomless riches of Christ;" – Ephesians 3:8

Paul, the man who brought the gospel to the world, considered himself to be the least of all the saints. It is this same attitude we should have in our daily walk with Christ.

We should not think more of ourselves than we should.

When we start feeling we are important in the grand scheme of things, let us compare ourselves to Jesus. We will see that He is so much more than we are, and in comparison to Him, we are nothing.

⁶ Blessed are those who thirst and have a strong desire for righteousness, for they shall be filled.

The Greek word (peináō) can be translated "hungry, hunger or to avidly or strongly desire something. In translating verse six for the TRIB™ translation, I chose "strong desire" rather than the traditional word "hunger", because I believe it expresses the true meaning of the desire that we should exhibit for righteousness.

If we do not eat or drink for a few days, we would experience a tolerable desire for food and water, yet we would still be searching very hard to find some. If we found nothing and another day or two passed by, the body would be screaming for food and water to the point you would almost kill to obtain it. This is the type of hunger God is looking for in us.

> "As the deer pants for the water brooks, so my soul pants after You, O God." – Psalm 42:1

Pant means to desire, cry or long for. The Psalmist so eloquently expresses his thirst for God by comparing it to a deer's thirst for water. The word of God makes the comparison of hungering and thirsting for something because water and food is to the physical body what righteousness is to our spiritual man inside us. The real you is covered by flesh. The real you is eternal and will spend an eternity either with Christ or in hell. It is this person we should concentrate on feeding. Our heavenly Father has promised to provide the necessary food and water for our fleshly body, leaving us with no worries or concerns outside of seeking the spiritual things to feed our inner man.

If we are to have a "strong desire" for righteousness, we must know what righteousness is. So, what is righteousness?

First, righteousness is imputed by God through the blood of Jesus Christ.

> "For He made *Jesus*, who knew no sin, to be sin on our behalf, so that we could be made the righteousness of God in Him." – 2 Corinthians 5:21

Our righteousness, or right standing with God, is made possible through salvation, by the blood of Jesus Christ. But righteousness is also a work.

> "But when the goodness and love of God our Savior appeared toward man, not by our works of righteousness, but by His mercy He saved us, by the baptism of rebirth and renewal of the Holy Ghost; which He abundantly shed on us through our Savior Jesus Christ; being justified by His grace, we

were made heirs according to the hope of eternal life." – Titus 3:4-7

Once we are saved, we are made righteous through the blood of Jesus. It is because our lives have changed and we are now in good standing with our heavenly Father that we do these righteous acts. This is what James was talking about when he stated:

> "Yes, someone may say, you have faith, and I have works: show me your faith without your works, and I will show you my faith by my works." – James 2:18

What are righteous acts? They are doing good things, such as feeding the poor, housing the homeless, giving money to your Church, helping someone mow their yard for free, and any other numerous good acts that you can think of. It is good things that God instructs us to do for our brothers and sisters, our neighbors or the stranger down the street. Just as God is righteous and does good things for us, we should do good things for others. It is because of God's righteousness that He has imputed on us through the blood of Jesus Christ that we desire to do these things.

> "For I say to you, that unless your righteousness shall go beyond that of the scribes and Pharisees, you shall not enter into the kingdom of heaven." – Matthew 5:20

The Pharisees were meticulous in performing their

righteous acts, such as paying tithes, performing ceremonial sacrifices, giving to the poor, etc. The difference in their righteous acts and ours is they did it for the praise of men. In order for ours to exceed theirs, we must always do it for the glory of God, not drawing any attention to ourselves.

OK, so let's recap!

1. To strongly desire and thirst for righteousness is to continually desire to be in a right standing relationship with God. To be outside of His will is an agonizing torment to those who seek God's righteousness.

2. Because of our relationship with God, and the continual seeking of His righteousness, we desire to perform righteous acts for His glory. A Christian should always be willing and looking to do good for others. These righteous acts cannot save us, and these acts are worthless compared to God's righteousness, but any child of God that seeks His righteousness will naturally strive to be righteous simply to be like Him.

3. Do not be proud or boastful of your righteousness. Doing good things for others is our Christian duty, it does not make us anything special. We are still not worthy of the grace and mercy that God bestows on us through His Son, Jesus Christ. So we must be careful that we do not think more of ourselves than we should.

⁷ Blessed are the merciful, for they shall be shown

mercy.

"He or she got what they deserved." How many times do we ourselves say something like that? It is really not too Christian of us. We ourselves have received an abundance of mercy from God our Father, and for us not to show the same mercy to others, regardless of race, creed, color, religion, etc., is not being very Christ like.

> "So when they continued to ask Him, He stood up and said to them, whoever is among you that is without sin, let him cast the first stone at her." – John 8:7

A woman caught in adultery was brought to Jesus by the Scribes and Pharisees trying to trick Jesus into saying something that would be contrary to the Law of Moses, but little did they know the joke would be on them.

When they pressed Jesus on the issue of what to do, the Law stated she had to die, He told them, "Whoever is without sin, cast the first stone." Of course, they all left one by one.

After they left, Jesus asked the woman, "Where are your accusers? Did no one condemn you?" The woman answers and says, "No one, Lord." Then Jesus said, "Neither do I, go and sin no more."

Talk about mercy. If anyone could have condemned her Jesus could, yet He chose to show mercy. Jesus set the example on what true mercy is, not only with the woman caught in adultery, but the very act of forgiving us of our sins and delivering us from the eternal punishment that we all deserve. We must show this type of mercy toward others, whether they are deserving or not, if we are to be true Disciples of Christ and sons and daughters of God.

⁸ Blessed are the pure in heart, for they shall see God.

To best understand the meaning of pure, let's look at its opposite, which is unclean, dirty, impure. Since this is dealing with the heart, we know Jesus was referring to spiritual pureness, not physical. So what are some things that can make one "not pure" spiritually?

1. Our Speech.

> "A good man out of the storeroom of his heart brings forth what is good; and the wicked man out of the storeroom of his heart brings forth what is evil: for out of the abundance of the heart his mouth speaks." – Luke 6:45

What's in the heart comes out the mouth. So a pure heart, or a clean heart, would never tell a dirty joke, insult someone, gossip about someone or ridicule someone. This is an indication that our heart is dirty and needs a good cleaning. A clean, purified heart will only speak uplifting, encouraging words that glorify God.

2. Our Hearing.

We must realize that what we allow ourselves to sit around and listen to feeds the heart and soul. For example; if we sit around in a room full of people who are constantly using profanity, we are more apt to slip up and say a profane word ourselves. It has happened to me before as I am sure it has happened to you also if you were ever in that situation.

The music we listen to, the television shows we watch, the movies we watch, the people we hang with all affect the purity of our heart. It is like we run our heart through a mud puddle when we allow our heart to listen to filth. And if something gets dirty, we must clean it. Which leads us up to the next question.

How do we make our heart pure?

We can't make our own heart pure, as it is something only God can do. The purification process is an ongoing daily process that is only accomplished by God's divine grace.

> "If we acknowledge our sins, He is faithful and righteous to forgive us our sins, and to cleanse us from all unrighteousness." – 1 John 1:9

The word "cleanse" is from the Greek word (katharizō) which means to make clean or purify. It is when we go to God in prayer that He makes us clean or purifies us by the precious blood of Jesus. We must continually, "daily", go to God in prayer to keep our hearts pure. Continually, with every opportunity throughout the day, we should also be feeding our heart the word of God. A heart that is full of the word of God can remain pure much longer than a heart that is void of the Word.

Because of this constant communication between us and God in order to keep our hearts pure, we build an intimate relationship with our Father. It is only when we have an intimate relationship with our Father that He reveals Himself to us, and we truly see God.

We should set aside a time each day that we know we will not be bothered by our worldly cares just to spend time with our heavenly Father. He longs to spend one on one quality time with you and me. He has promised to draw close to us if we will only draw close to Him.

> "Draw near to God, and He will draw near to you. Cleanse your hands you sinners; and purify your hearts you double minded." – James 4:8

⁹ Blessed is the peacemaker, for he shall be called the son of God.

A child of God not only loves peace, they do everything within their power to make peace.

Being a peacemaker is saying "I apologize" even when you are not the one in the wrong.

Being a peacemaker is bringing a sinner to Christ. By doing so, we have made peace between man and God.

Being a peacemaker is helping others make peace with themselves or someone else.

As a reward of being a peacemaker, we are called the sons of God. We have shown that we serve the Prince of Peace, Jesus Christ.

> "Peace I leave with you; My peace I give to you; I do not give to you peace like the world gives. Do not let your heart be troubled, nor let it be afraid." – John 14:27

It is the peace that Jesus gave to us that we should strive to show and give to others. We, as believers, have a peace the world does not understand. Even in times of extreme adversity, we exhibit a peace that makes others notice there is something different about us. It is our duty and honor to give that kind of peace to someone else.

10 Blessed are those who are persecuted for righteousness sake, for the kingdom of heaven is theirs.

If we are truly living by all the words that Jesus spoke within these three chapters, we will be persecuted. It is not an "if" or a "maybe", it is a definite.

> "Yes, all who wish to live a godly life in Christ Jesus will suffer persecution." – 2 Timothy 3:12

When we no longer hang with our old friends, no longer participate in the dirty jokes, no longer go to the places we use to and no longer seem to be the same old person, the world will notice. When Jesus has truly made a change, you will be persecuted because of Him.

We do not see much persecution in the United States. It is not because we are a godly nation and have God's hand of protection on us, it is because our Christians are worldly.

¹¹ Blessed are you when others insult you and persecute you, and lie and say all kinds of evil words against you on account of Me. ¹² Rejoice and be extremely joyful, for your reward is great in heaven. In this manner they persecuted the prophets who were before you.

We will be insulted, lied on, people saying all kinds of evil things about us, all because of who we serve. If everyone around us is saying nothing but good things about us that is an indicator that we are not living a godly life. Of course, we are not to purposely set out to make people say bad things or use Jesus just to irritate people.

> "Therefore, go out from among them and be separate, says the Lord, and do not touch that which is unclean, and I will accept you." – 2 Corinthians 6:17

God expects us to separate ourselves from the world. If we have fully conformed to His word, we will be different than the world, and this can cause them to hate us, insult us, and persecute us and the like. Have you ever seen a young kid make fun of someone else that is different? It is in our sinful nature to single out those that are different than ourselves and to do all kinds of cruel things to them.

> "You adulterers and adulteresses, do you not know that friendship with the world is hostility toward God? Whoever will be a friend with the world is the enemy of God." – James 4:4

We cannot be friends with the world or otherwise we make ourselves an enemy to God. Again, I cannot stress enough, if we are living by the words of Christ in these three chapters, we will not be a friend to the world, but we will be its enemy, and with such persecution comes. However, we are to rejoice and be extremely joyful when persecution comes, because we have some awesome rewards waiting for us in heaven. If that doesn't make you want to praise the Lord, nothing will.

13 You are the salt of the earth, but if the salt loses its saltiness, how can it be made salty again? It is therefore good for nothing except to be thrown outside and trampled under the feet of men.

14 You are the light of the world. A city set on a mountain cannot be hid. 15 Nor do they light a lamp and put it under a bucket, but on a lampstand, and it shines for all who are in the house. 16 Let your light shine before men, so they may see your good works and praise your Father who is in heaven.

A true believer in Christ never has to broadcast that he is a Christian, it shows from the life he is living. It is not something that he can hide either, because "a city set on a mountain cannot be hid."

> "It so happen, when Moses came down from Mount Sinai, (the two tablets of testimony were in his hands as he came down from the mountain), that Moses did not know that the skin on his face was radiant with light because he had been talking with God." – Exodus 34:39

Just like Moses, when a believer spends time talking with God, it will show on his face. Our time spent talking with God is the most valuable time of the day. It is the believer's source of power. For any light to shine, it has to have a power source. When we spend time on our knees or prostrate before God talking with Him, the Holy Spirit becomes the power source that powers our light that shines. Now equip that same believer with the word of God, Satan and every demon around trembles when he or she wakes up each morning.

"The object of our shining is not that men may see how good we are, nor even see us at all, but that they may see grace in us and God in us, and cry, 'What a Father these people must have.' Is not this the first time in the New Testament that God is called our Father? Is it not singular that the first time it peeps out should be when men are seeing the good works of his children?" (Spurgeon)

¹⁷ Do not think that I have come to abolish the Law or the Prophets. I came not to abolish, but to complete *it*. ¹⁸ For verily I say to you, till heaven and earth pass away, not one stroke of the smallest letter shall pass from the law until all is accomplished. ¹⁹ Therefore, whoever dismisses one of the least of these commandments and teaches men to do so shall be called the least in the kingdom of heaven. But whoever practices and teaches them, he will be called great in the kingdom of God.

Jesus accomplished what no other possibly could, He lived every "stroke of the smallest letter" of the law perfectly. Though He was often accused by the scribes and Pharisees of breaking the law, Jesus always showed the true meaning of what God intended in the Law.

For the rest of this chapter, Jesus sets out to show the true meaning of the Law of Moses that the Scribes and Pharisees had interpreted all wrong. Just because we received salvation through Jesus does not mean that we are lawless. We do have commandments to keep. Jesus said:

> "If you love me, you will keep my commandments."
> – John 14:15

Jesus' commandments are rules for living, not a set of burdensome laws that no man could ever keep, as was the Law of Moses. And if we truly love Jesus, we will obey His commandments. When we are obedient to Christ commands, He works in our lives in ways we could never dream. It is the obedient child that receives the blessings of God.

> "And Samuel said, Does Yahweh have as much pleasure in burnt offerings and sacrifices as He does in obeying His voice? Behold, to obey is better than sacrifice and to carefully listen than the fat of rams."
> – 1 Samuel 15:22

20 For I say to you, that unless your righteousness shall go beyond that of the scribes and Pharisees, you shall not enter into the kingdom of heaven.

The Scribes were those who were employed in the handwriting of the scriptures and expounding on the Law of Moses. The Pharisees were the strictest of all the religious sects in Israel at the time. They outwardly and publicly displayed their acts of righteousness, such as sacrifices, paying tithes and saying long prayers in public, but they were not sincere in their hearts. They only longed for the praise of men, not the praise of God.

The Scribes were like many of our modern day Scholars. They could translate scripture and expound upon the laws of God, but their knowledge of God was all intellectual knowledge, not a knowledge that was learnt on their knees, with much prayer, by the Holy Spirit.

We must not desire the praises of men, as the Pharisees and we must have a "heart" knowledge of God, not just a head knowledge as the Scribes. Our righteousness must be more than these two groups or we will not inherit the kingdom of God. And without a doubt, these two groups were 100% dedicated at what they did, but all for the wrong reasons. Let's make sure our 100% dedication is all for the right reasons.

21 You have heard that it was said to those of long ago, "You shall not commit murder", and whoever murders will be subject to the judgment. 22 But I say to you, that whoever is angry with his brother without reason is in danger of the judgment. And whoever shall insult his brother shall be in danger of the Sanhedrin. But whoever shall say, "You worthless fool!" shall be in danger of hell fire.

The Pharisees and the Law of Moses taught that murder consisted of taking someone's life. Jesus extended the act of murder to the anger felt in the heart toward someone. Jesus was in fact saying, "The unjustified anger that was in the heart that prompted the murder was just as bad as the murder itself." We see Jesus applying the same concept to adultery a little later on. What we secretly hold in our heart and meditate upon can be just as sinful as doing the act itself, as we are sinning against God, not man. When we physically commit the act we meditated on, then it becomes a sin against man. Either way results in sin.

> "And He said, "It is that which comes out of the man that defiles the man. For from inside the heart of men proceed evil thoughts, adulteries,

fornications, murders, thefts, greediness, wickedness, deceit, sexual excess, wishing others injury because of envy, blasphemy, *and* pride: All these evil things come from inside and defile the man." – Mark 7:20-23

All of those things are sins that are first committed in the heart and then physically committed. A thought becomes sin when it is contemplated on how you can achieve such a thing without getting caught or the pleasure such a thing would bring. It is for this reason the Apostle Paul instructs us to:

> "Casting down imaginations, and every arrogant thing that elevates itself against the knowledge of God, and take captive every thought to the obedience of Christ." – 2 Corinthians 10:5

We cannot help what Satan throws into our minds that is evil, but we can help the thoughts that we entertain. We are instructed to "cast down" those thoughts immediately, not to sit and entertain them. This takes a conscious effort on our part, especially if we are the daydreaming type. It is easy to entertain the thought of sin. Satan cannot read our mind, so we have to verbally rebuke the thoughts that he places there. Do not just try to ignore those thoughts, rebuke them verbally in the name of Jesus. Get rid of that sin before it can ever make itself home inside your heart.

23 Therefore, if you offer your gift at the altar and remember that your brother has something against

you; ²⁴ **leave your gift in front of the altar and leave. First make peace with your brother and then come back and offer your gift.**

Here Jesus shows the importance of mending relationships before we engage in any type of religious duty.

Who is our brother? Who is our Sister?

A person who is not a believer in Christ is not our brother or sister, although we often hear many proclaim, "We are all brothers and sisters", or "We are all God's children", trying to include those who do not believe in Christ also. God is not the Father of unbelievers, because it is only those who receive Jesus who He gives the power to become sons and daughters of God.

> "But to all who received Him and believed on His name, to them He gave the power to become the sons of God." – John 1:12

Many believe that "we are all God's children" because He created us all, but that is not the case. God only took part in two creations, the first being Adam and the second being Jesus, the rest of us are created by man. Both creations God took part in were created without sin, and that just cannot be said of us. It is because we are created by a fleshly fallen Father and Mother, using the process that God designed, that we are sinful.

To be considered a child of God involves being born a second time, and this birth is the creation of God through

Jesus Christ our Lord. As Jesus told Nicodemus, "Unless a man is born again he cannot see the kingdom of God". Jesus goes on to say, "that which is born of the flesh is flesh, but that which is born of the Spirit is spirit." (John Chapter 3) We go from man's creation to God's creation when we accept the sacrifice Jesus offered for the remission of our sins. You must be God's creation to be considered His child. If you are not God's creation, you are not part of His family, but the family of Satan. It is a horrible thought to think that your spouse, your child, your father or your mother is the child of Satan, but it is scriptural truth. Therefore, we must pray that much more for our families to accept what the precious blood of Jesus offers: "The right to be called the child of God."

Now, let's move on to what Jesus is teaching in this passage of scripture. As brothers and sisters in Christ, we will often have disagreements and hard feelings with one another, just as Paul and Barnabas had over John Mark rejoining them in their travels. (Acts 15:39)

Here, Jesus is telling us to mend those relationships with our brothers and sisters in Christ, as well as our biological brothers and sisters, before we offer anything to God. As stated in the "Blessed are the..." portion at the beginning of this chapter, sometimes we have to apologize even when we are not in the wrong just to restore peace in a relationship, then leave it up to God to settle your wrong with the other party.

25 Settle your case with your accuser quickly, while you are on the way to the magistrate; so that your accuser does not hand you over to the judge, and the judge to the officer, and *the officer* throw you into prison. 26 Verily I say to you, "You will not come out from there till you have paid the last penny."

Jesus gives us a parable on the urgency to settle bad relationships. Paul tells us the same when he wrote, "Be angry and do not sin: do not let the sun set on your anger." (Ephesians 4:26)

Broken relationships that are not immediately fixed hinders your relationship with Jesus and the person with whom you have a grievance. In the parable, Jesus is using the illustration of settling your grievance before it goes to court. We must be careful not to let things go too far before we decide to settle the dispute with our brother or it could become very hard to mend the relationship. Rule of thumb: "The quicker, the better." This will make like the third time I have said this, and it probably will not be the last – "Sometimes we must apologize even when we are not the one at fault just to make peace because that is the Christian thing to do." I am not saying we must lie and say we are in the wrong when we are not, but a simple, "I apologize, I do not want to have any hard feelings with you." will suffice.

27 You have heard that it was said to those of long ago, "You shall not commit adultery." 28 But I say to

you, that all who look upon a woman to lust after her has already committed adultery with her in his heart.

In the Old Testament it was all about earthly things. God's covenant with His people were earthly things, such as land flowing with milk and honey and wealth. The New Testament on the other hand is all about the heavenly things. For example, we are instructed to lay up our treasures in heaven, whereas in the Old Testament, treasures and the spoils of war were stored here on earth. Sins are no longer just physical acts as in the Old Testament, but now are motives of the heart.

The sin of adultery is now a matter of the heart also. To even look upon a woman with lust in your heart while married is adultery. In our society today, most believe its ok to look as long as you do not touch. Of course, we can see this is contrary to the teachings of Jesus.

Trying to find a place to look in public without spotting a model in her panties and bra is getting to be almost impossible. Satan has given men, especially, every opportunity to lust after another woman. Television is just as bad. If you do find a clean show you can watch with the family, you will be met with a Victoria Secret commercial or other adult products that can entice you to think upon things that are sinful. We almost have to lock ourselves in our bedroom and not come out to avoid the temptation to lust. So what's a man to do? Move to a Muslim country where all the women are clothed from head to toe?

The solution lies within these three chapters, it is called prayer. And it is found in what we call the "Lord's Prayer". In one portion of the prayer it states, "Lead me not into temptation." Jesus was showing us how to pray, as we will see a little later. We are to pray that God will lead us in a different path that does not lead to temptation. And guess what? If you ask Him to He will. But that does not mean that we will never be tempted, because we will. But we are promised that with every temptation, God will make a way to overcome it.

> "There is no temptation that has overtaken you except that which belongs to man; and God is trustworthy, who will not allow you to be tempted above what you are able *to withstand*, but will with every temptation also make a way for you to escape, that you may be able to endure it." – 1 Corinthians 10:13

When we find ourselves tempted, we should first pray for the Lord's assistance in overcoming the temptation, rebuke the enemy in the name of Jesus and then remove ourselves from the source of temptation as quickly as possible. If we have to walk looking at the ground, then so be it. If we have to quit watching television, then so be it. And that really is not a bad idea given all the filth on it anymore. As the days grow increasingly wicked and lawless, we must draw closer to God, asking Him to keep our hearts pure and our eyes fixed solely upon Jesus. Meditating on the word of God, which shields our hearts and minds from the fiery darts of the enemy.

[29] If your right eye causes you to sin, pluck it out and throw it away from you. For it is better for you that one of your members should perish, than for your whole body to be cast into hell. [30] If your right hand causes you to sin, cut it off and throw it away from you. For it is better for you that one member of your body perish, than for your whole body to be cast into hell.

Here, Jesus teaches that lust is no joking matter. It will land your whole body in hell, to burn forever. If someone just cannot keep from lusting, Jesus prescribes a very harsh remedy to deal with the lust, which is to discard the offending body part, such as the eye or the hand. The hand if it can't keep from stealing and the like.

Most Scholars and Bible Commentators claim Jesus is speaking figuratively or spiritually here, that He would never instruct us to engage in self-mutilation. But nowhere does the text imply that it is figurative or spiritual, but I would agree that it would be the very last resort one would consider.

If walking with your head down, closing your eyes, looking the other way, spending hours in prayer and fasting, going before the Church and having them pray, if none of these things bring deliverance, then it is better to rid yourself of that body part than to go to hell. Again, many would disagree with me, and if you do that is ok, but personally, I would gladly rid myself of a body part if it would keep me out of hell. We should serve Jesus because He is worthy and we love Him, not just to avoid hell, but hell is definitely a deterrent to sin and should be avoided by any means necessary. Don't you agree?

The Greek word used for hell in these two verses is γέεννα (géenna) lit. Gehenna. It is mentioned twelve times in the New Testament, and eleven out of those twelve was used by Jesus Himself.

The Greek word Gehenna actually refers to the "Valley of Hinnom". In biblical times, it was a valley that lied just outside the walls of Jerusalem and it was used to dump garbage and human bodies. A fire constantly burned there, thus the reason Jesus used it to compare the final destiny of those who would reject Him and enjoy living in sinful fleshly lust. It is the final dwelling place of Satan, his angels and demons, and those who reject Christ. It is the lake of fire.

It is no wonder Jesus said it would be better to lose a body part than spend an eternity in the lake of fire. But losing a body part is not necessary, because God will deliver us "from the sin that so easily entangles us" if we will only put our trust in Jesus. Sin is serious and we should not take it lightly. God hates sin and so should we. We should not accept sin because it may be the politically correct thing to do. Make a decision today to no longer tolerate sin in your life. It may mean losing friends, family or what you consider fun, but ask yourself, is a life of pleasure and friendship with sin worth an eternity in hell? I think we both know the answer to that.

Jesus Teaches About Divorce
(Matthew 19:1-12; Mark 10:1-12; Luke 16:18)

31 It was also said, "Whoever divorces his wife, let him give her a written notice of divorce." 32 But I say to you that whoever divorces his wife for any reason other than sexual immorality causes her to commit adultery. And whoever marries a woman who has been put away commits adultery.

The first thing we notice here is Jesus didn't say, "You have heard that it was said by those "long ago"". It wasn't the Law of Moses that Jesus was referencing, but an allowance by the Pharisees. It had gotten to the point that if a man got bored with his wife or just didn't like her any longer, he could divorce her.

"But I say to you" – Jesus wasn't telling them anything new, He was explaining what the Law intended all along, that marriage should be forever, except if one of the two broke the marriage covenant by cheating with another person, simply put, committing adultery.

Can the innocent party ever remarry? Catholicism says, "No, he and/or she can never remarry, even if their spouse committed adultery and they were released from the marriage according to scripture." Greek and Protestant Churches argue that on the grounds of adultery, the innocent party can remarry. Should the innocent party seek to remarry?

According to the Apostle Paul, it is better to remain single so you can solely dedicate yourself to Christ. (1 Corinthians 7:8) So, if you are single now and want to totally commit yourself to the work of Christ, how can I disagree with Paul? But if you cannot handle being alone without a mate, the Apostle Paul said it is better to marry than to burn with lust. (1 Corinthians 7:9) We seen in previous scripture where those who lust end up.

To those who have been a victim of adultery, I would give the same advice as the Apostle Paul. If you can handle not having another mate and being alone, it is best to remain single so you can place your sole attention upon Jesus and serving Him. But being alone is not for everyone and the scriptures do not say it is a sin to remarry if your spouse has cheated on you or has left you for someone else. So if you cannot handle being alone, pray for the will of God in your life. Make sure it is His will you remarry. If it is, wait on Him to send you someone else, do not, because of loneliness, find someone of your own choosing and risk causing tragedy in your life once again. Marriage is "till death do you part" and if you make a bad choice, they are not returnable and have no trade in value. You are simply stuck with a lemon for the rest of your life. If you already have a lemon, be of good cheer, God is good at making lemonade for those who love Him and are called according to His purpose.

Jesus Teaches About Swearing Oaths

[33] Again, you have heard that it was said by those of long ago, "You shall not swear falsely, but shall repay your oaths to the Lord." [34] But I say to you not to swear at all. Not by heaven, for it is God's throne, [35] and not by the earth, for it is His footstool. Nor by Jerusalem, for it is the city of the Great King. [36] Neither shall you swear by your head, because you are not able to make one hair white or black. [37] But let your answer be Yes or No. For anything more than this is evil.

When someone does not believe what we are saying, it is natural to say, "I swear I am not lying." But Jesus instructs us to not swear at all, and he is not talking about using profanity. We must train ourselves to let others believe what we say or not believe, it's their choice.

> "But above all things, my brothers, do not swear by heaven, or by the earth, or by any other oath: let your yes be yes; and your no be no; lest you fall into judgment." – James 5:12

The need to swear or make an oath on our part, beyond a simple yes or no, shows the worthlessness of our own words. It shows that our character is such that people will not believe what we say unless we are appealing to something or someone greater than ourselves. If our character is good, then our word is good and never questioned.

"Lest you fall into judgment." – By having to swear or take an oath, thus showing our bad character, we risk being judged for that lack of character on judgment day. If people think so little of our word, apparently we haven't been living the life Christ instructed us to. That is why it is so important to speak honestly with everyone. I know it is an old saying, but it still rings just as true today, "A man is only as good as his word." And that goes for women too.

> "Do not fear those who can kill the body but are not able to kill the soul: but rather fear Him who is able to destroy both soul and body in hell." – Matthew 10:28

When we do not fear or care what man thinks, we have no need to lie. It is because we have done something we shouldn't have and afraid of getting caught or we care what someone thinks that we lie. When we can get to a place in our life where we neither fear man nor care what man thinks of us, we eliminate our reasons to lie. That is not to say we will never lie again. As long as we are in this fleshly body we will sin, but lying should be but such a rare occasion that even you will be amazed it slipped out of your mouth.

As a Christian honesty shouldn't even be an issue, yet there is just as much dishonesty in the Church today as there is in the world. Once we are labeled as a dishonest person, then we find ourselves in the position of having to swear or take an oath for others to believe us. Any new convert should start day one making a conscious effort to speak honestly with others regardless of the situation. We need to start our children off at a young age showing them the importance of telling the truth and not trying to hide the fact that they have done wrong. But most importantly, we need to lead by example, letting our life be a reflection of how to live for Christ.

38 You have heard that it was said, "An eye for an eye and a tooth for a tooth." 39 But I say to you, "Do not oppose someone evil, and if someone slaps you on your right cheek, turn to him the other also."

A command of Jesus that very few keep. Most jokingly say, "It doesn't say what to do after you turn the other cheek." Or others say, "God doesn't expect us to be anybody's doormat." Really? Can you show me that passage in the word of God? Public humiliation is something most of us do not tolerate nor handle well, and I have to be honest and say I have problems in this area also.

It is humiliating for someone to degrade us in public and not defend ourselves. It is humiliating for someone to slap or punch us and look cowardly in front of everyone, including our family. Your wife or girlfriend will not think you are much of a man if you are a coward, the devil tells us. What will my children think of me? I will be an embarrassment and a shame to them if I do not fight back. It all comes down to pride.

"It was pride that changed angels into devils." – Augustine of Hippo

And it is pride that will do the same to you and me. This wasn't Jesus just making a suggestion, nor is it one of those things we can elect to keep if we feel like it. Jesus said, "If you love me, you will keep my commandments", (John 14:15) and this is one of those commandment.

What does it mean, "Do not oppose someone evil"? It means that we sit, without opposition, and take what they are dishing out to us. I can see the pride swelling up in you now and saying to yourself, "This preacher isn't playing with a bag full of marbles if he thinks I am going to sit and take stuff off of others. That isn't what this scripture is saying at all." So, what is it saying then? Look at when Jesus was arrested before His crucifixion, from that point forward, and tell me Jesus didn't live the example for us. They ridiculed and mocked Him, they beat Him and abused Him and what did He do in return? Nothing. Jesus didn't instruct us to do something here that He didn't first do Himself.

We need to pray, fast and meditate upon the word of God until every last ounce of pride is taken from us. God hasn't yet perfected me in this area, but I try with all that is within me to honor His word and I pray and repent for my shortcomings. My dear brothers and sisters, we can say we love Jesus all day long, but if we purposefully ignore and not keep one of His commandments, we do not love Him. Father, in the name of Jesus, help us to be more like your Son and our Redeemer. Please, we cry out with all that is within us, take away this filthy pride that keeps us from pleasing you.

40 And if anyone wants to sue you and take away your shirt, let him have your coat also. 41 And whoever forces you to go one mile, go with him two. 42 Give to the one who demands you to, and from the one who wants to borrow from you, do not say no.

Here again are some very hard commands for us to keep. Here is a command not to fight someone in court, but let them have what they are suing you for and more. Once again, people go kicking and screaming trying to spiritualize these commands to mean something they do not simply because they do not want to do what Jesus instructed them to do.

Secondly, if we are forced to go with someone against our will, not only go with them, but go above and beyond what they demand of you.

"Give to the one who demands you to." – If someone demands that you give them something of yours, you do not pull out your concealed carry 9mm handgun and put a hole in them, you give them what they are demanding of you. And if someone wants to borrow something from you, do not tell them no.

These are very grievous commands for most of us. Again, they are commands that most of us will try to explain away because we think that it is unreasonable for Jesus to ask such things of us, so it has to mean something different. It would be very difficult for me to loan someone my Google Nexus 7 tablet or my laptop that I am using to write this book, just for the asking. And that is why I will not let my children read this portion of the book. Ha ha!

Seriously, these are commands that we must read literally and take at face value. They need no interpretation, just obedience. When we indeed live according to Jesus' commandments, all of a sudden our Christian walk gets a whole lot harder.

43 You have heard that it was said, "You shall love your neighbor and hate your enemy." 44 But I say to you, "Love your enemies, bless those who curse you, do well to those who hate you, and pray for those who abuse you and persecute you, 45 that you may become sons of your Father who is in heaven.

Love our enemies, bless someone who is cursing us, do good things for those who hate us, and pray for those who abuse and persecute us. That is one tall glass of water to drink for the most dedicated Christian, but yet Jesus commands us to do those things. How can we accomplish such noble feats as Jesus did?

Can you think of anyone, off the top of your head that really loves their enemies, or if they were getting cussed out in a Wal-Mart line for having twenty-one items in the twenty item lane, would turn around and bestow a blessing upon that person? No, most of us would turn around and give them a piece of our mind or better yet, punch them in the face. And if we did pray, it would be for ten thousand fleas to infest their armpit.

The truth is, we don't see Christians that walk like Christ did too often in our lifetime. I wish I could say, as the Apostle Paul, "Therefore, I exhort you, imitate me" (1 Corinthians 4:16), but I stand before you ashamed that I can't. We think of most bible commentators as very righteous men that has attained full knowledge of the word of God, but the truth is, we are human and have a lot of the same faults you do. Do I earnestly try to keep the commands of Christ? Yes, with my utmost! Do I fail Christ? More often than I would like to admit. But, if we are to please God, we will keep these commandments of Jesus.

People make it hard to love them. It seems the better you are to someone, the more they try to walk on you. That is because Satan sees your obedience to Christ as weakness, but what he doesn't realize is this:

> "For this reason I take pleasure in weakness, in insults, in trouble, in persecutions, in difficulties for Christ's sake, for when I am weak, then am I

strong." – 2 Corinthians 12:10

Our weakness allows the strength of Christ to work in us. Satan doesn't realize that our obedience to Christ is our strength, not our weakness.

My Dad told me a story of when he was in the military. My Dad is 6'-2" tall and stout as a bull. He thought this midget that was mouthing him would be easy to shut-up with a well-placed fist upside his head. He said that midget had fist coming from every direction. He was in front of him, then behind him, then beside him and he just couldn't keep up with that little guy. My Dad said he finally threw up his hands and said, "I have had enough" and walked off, leaving that midget to bask in his victory.

Satan does like my dad did, he underestimates us because we look small when we are being obedient to Christ commands. But wasn't it a young man named David who killed a giant? God takes small things to do big things. He takes the weak things to show His strength. He takes the shy person and makes them bold. He takes the quietest person to speak the loudest through.

The only way we can love our enemies, bestow a blessing on someone that is cursing us or genuinely pray for those who abuse us and persecute us is to allow Jesus do it through us. There is no way we can do it on our own. That is why a relationship with Christ is essential if we are to keep His commandments and be like Him. You will be sick of hearing me say this by the time you reach the end

of this book, but if we love Jesus, we
_____. I think you know the rest of it.

For He causes His sun to rise on the evil and the good, and sends rain on the just and the unjust. ⁴⁶ For if you love those who love you, what reward do you have? Do not even the tax collectors do the same? ⁴⁷ And if you greet your brothers only, do you do any more than others? Do not even the tax collectors do the same? ⁴⁸ You, therefore, must be perfect, even as your Father in heaven is perfect.

Loving those that love us comes pretty easy most of the time. But loving someone who is a continual pain in our backside is another thing altogether, and it seems those are the type of people we attract as Christians. It is Jesus giving us every opportunity to love those who drive us crazy.

I remember watching "A Thief in the Night" rapture movie series that came out in 1972. In one of the movie's it pictured a room full of Christian's clothed in white robes, waiting for their turn to get their head chopped off, singing, "they will know we are Christian's by our love." To love the unlovable is the trademark of being a disciple of Christ. If we are not capable of doing that, then the love of Christ is not in us.

I say the "love of Christ is not us" because to be able to love unconditionally, those that are unlovable, is not a human trait, it's a Jesus trait. I can't love a pedophile, but Jesus can. I can't love someone who kills their parents, but Jesus can. There are a lot of people in this world I cannot love, it takes the God kind of love to do that, and it's only available through Jesus Christ.

There are three words in the Greek that deal with love:

agapáō [to love], agápē [love], agapētós [beloved]

Agapáō (verb) – To agapáō something means to totally be committed to something; or to be totally consumed by it. What we agapáō we put first in our lives. Such as you cannot agapáō God and worldly wealth, which we will study in Chapter 6. You will be totally committed to either God or your money, not both. This is what agapáō love is.

Agápē (noun) – Unlike agapáō, agápē is never used in a negative sense. That is because it is the unconditional love that can only come from God. It is the love that flows inside of us once we receive Christ as our Savior and Redeemer. It is the type of love that is able to love the unlovable.

We can do none of these commandments without

allowing Christ to operate through us. We can't do these commandments without having a close relationship with Jesus. We can't do these commandments without the Holy Spirit operating in us. We cannot do these commandments ourselves. Without the "God" kind of love, we cannot love others like Jesus is telling us to. We must be closer to Christ than we are the world for the Holy Spirit to operate in us like Jesus commands. This relationship is built over time with many hours of prayer, many hours of studying the word of God and many hours proving to God that a relationship with Him is more important than anything in your life. With some, this takes a year or two, others it takes a lifetime, and sadly some never develop a relationship with Christ at all.

The most important thing about building a relationship with Christ is not to get discouraged. It does not happen minutes after your get saved. Just as with a spouse, the first few years are a little rocky as you get to know Him better and learn His likes and dislikes (which is the purpose of this book). The longer you spend with Him, the more you get to know Him and then a relationship starts to form from which miracles flow. Do not let the devil get you discouraged.

    "Draw near to God, and He will draw near to

you. Cleanse your hands, you sinners; and purify your hearts you double minded." – James 4:8

He promised if we draw close to Him, He will, in return, draw close to us. Put your trust and faith in Him and build that relationship that will last for all eternity.

"You, therefore, must be perfect, even as your Father in heaven is perfect." – We will never be able to be perfect until Jesus returns and we are given new bodies that knows no sin. But, Jesus instructs us to strive for that perfection while still here on earth. He demands perfection of us.

Can we go without sin for an entire day, week or month? Yes, our walk should not be filled with continual sinning. There are days we will slip up and not do what Christ has instructed us, but it should not be daily. But this comes with time and a relationship that is built with Christ through many trials and tribulations.

As a new Christian, it will seem like every time you turn around you have done something wrong. This is normal. Just ask for forgiveness, learn from your mistake and move on. Do not let the devil beat you down and make you feel like a failure, urging you to throw in the towel. As you grow in Christ, you will sin less, but you will never be without sin while still in the fleshly body you are in.

If you have children, you know there are days they seem like angels, doing everything you ask and behaving as an obedient child should. Then there are days they are one hundred percent brats. But they eventually learn over time, with much correction, how to behave.

As a "newborn" believer, we have to first be bottle fed, then we start to crawl, then we start walk, then we are walking good, but we still stumble and fall at times. But as we grow and develop balance and coordination, we stumble and fall a whole lot less. Jesus has very high expectations of us and we should strive to be perfect, but on those rare occasions we stumble, Jesus is there to pick us up and forgive us. He will say to us as He said to the adulterous woman, "I do not condemn you. Go, and do not sin again." (John 8:1-11)

CHAPTER 6

¹ Be careful not to do your charitable giving *openly* before men *only* to be seen by them. Otherwise, you have no reward from your Father who is in heaven. ² Therefore, when you do your charitable giving, do not sound a trumpet before you as the hypocrites do in the synagogues and in the streets, that they may receive praise from men. Truly, I say to you, they have been given their reward. ³ But when you do charitable giving, do not let your left hand know what your right hand is doing, ⁴ that you're charitable giving may be in secret. And your Father, who sees what you done in secret, will Himself reward you openly.

"Do not sound a trumpet before you as the hypocrites." This is referring to the Pharisees who liked to be seen by everyone whenever they did anything religious. They were like our large businesses and celebrities who have their, "I donated $1,000,000 to a homeless child shelter", promoted in press releases and broadcasted on national news, because it's good PR.

This is not talking about giving to your Church in the offering, this is talking about giving to the poor. Although, we should be very discreet on how we give our money in the offering plate also.

Having been an usher in a fairly good sized Church before when I was just starting out in the ministry, I had the privilege of passing the plate. Most who gave large offerings made sure the "20, 50 or 100" were showing on the bill when they placed it in the offering plate. Those who gave "1's or 5's" usually made sure the number was not showing and they were usually folded tightly and placed in the plate with the number facing down or scrunched up in a ball. While I didn't know the givers heart when they flaunted the amount, there is a difference in how those with money and those without place their offerings in the plate. If you are an usher at your church, start paying attention.

I, personally, am against passing offering plates for this reason and;

> "Let each one give as he purposes in his heart, not with regret or due to feeling pressured, because God loves a cheerful giver." – 2 Corinthians 9:7

If you do not have money to put in the offering plate and the usher hands it to you to pass or looks at you while walking by, it is very humiliating. This results in people feeling they have to put something in or risk looking bad to people around them. I do not feel this type of collection is biblical, but of course, I do not condemn churches for doing it this way because it's just tradition.

The biblical way, in my opinion, is to have a collection box with a slit in the top somewhere close to the entrance of the sanctuary. As people are entering or leaving, they can drop their offering in. Those who have it to give can do so discretely and those who do not have it are not pressured into giving or feeling bad when they can't.

But most churches will continue to have offering plates, so I suggest using an envelope or making you a money ball, like those who give dollars, if you plan on giving large denomination bills. Any type of giving you do, whether in church or outside the church should be done as much in secret as possible. We should never try to draw attention to ourselves. This includes talking to family and friends about what you give to others. What you give to God is between Him, your spouse and you, and it should not go any further or your reward will be the recognition you get from man, which results in no recognition from God.

Jesus Teaches About Prayer
(Luke 11:2-4)

5 When you pray, do not be as the hypocrites. For they love to pray standing in the synagogues and on the street corners so they may be seen by men. Truly, I say to you, they have been given their reward. 6 But you, when you pray, go to your private room. And when you have shut the door, pray to your Father in secret. And when you're Father, who sees what you done in secret, will Himself reward you openly.

If you attend a smaller church as I do, most have a prayer request segment where you can voice any urgent needs or prayers for healing for yourself or other family and friends you might have. Then whoever is leading this segment prays out loud, as do everyone else in the church. This scripture is not talking about this type of public prayer, nor is it talking about prayer at sporting events, etc.

You have probably seen videos on television or pictures of Jews praying at the Wailing Wall in Jerusalem. Let's say for instance there are 5 people standing fairly close to each other and one man is extremely loud in his prayer while the other four are relatively quiet and trying to remain secretive. Which one is the hypocrite? Yes, the one praying very loudly trying to draw attention to the fact that he is praying and how holy he is for doing so. It is this type of public display of prayer that these passages are referring to.

But, when possible, you should be at home in a private room where it's only you and God alone. One, you can pour out your heart without feeling like someone is standing over you listening. Two, this makes you much more relaxed so you can enjoy your time with your heavenly Father.

Those who _____ Jesus keeps His commandments. If we do not keep His commandments, we do not _____ Him. I know, I know. I repeat that way too much. But if you walk away from this book knowing anything, it will be that if you do not keep His commandments, you do not love Jesus.

7 When you pray, do not repeat the same words as the worldly do. For they believe they will be heard

**for their many words. ⁸ Therefore, do not be like
them. For your Father knows what you have need of
before you ask Him.**

There are several good nuggets of truth in verses seven and
eight. "When you pray, do not repeat the same words as
the worldly do." This is referencing a chant or saying the
same words over and over thinking this is somehow going
to get God to hear them. Jesus says do not be like them.

I do believe I understand the reasoning behind this, as do
anyone that has children. Have you ever had your child
repeat the same word or phrase over and over and over
again? Man sakes alive that can drive you bonkers. And
that very annoying word, "Why", with everything you say.
Saying the same thing over and over is not communicating,
it is irritating. God wants you to communicate from the
heart, not with a chant or a canned ritualistic prayer.

Our Father knows what we have need of before we ask, so
why ask? One of the main reasons is this scripture:

> "You lust and do not have: you kill and desire to
> have, yet you cannot obtain: you clash severely and
> wage war, **yet you do not have, because you do
> not ask.**" – James 4:2

We do not have things from God because we do not ask
Him for the things we need, we usually ask Him for the
things we greed. But regardless, our Father wants us to ask
Him for things. You know your child wants candy when

you go to the store, but you do not always get it for him unless he ask, then you decide if he has had enough sweets for the day or if his request is fine. Our heavenly Father works in a lot the same way. But where we will give in to our children's greed, God does not.

If we pay attention to the scripture, it says that God knows what we have "NEED" of before we ask. You will not always get your prayer answered because your perception of what you need and God's perception is totally different. I actually praise God for all the prayers He didn't answer when I look back over my life. So do not be disappointed if you ask for something and God's reply is no.

Next, Jesus teaches us how to pray in order to avoid those dreaded no's.

⁹ Therefore, pray in this way:

> **"Our Father who is in heaven, Holy is your name.**
> **¹⁰ Your kingdom come, Your will be done, on earth as it is in heaven.**
> **¹¹ Give us this day our daily bread.**
> **¹² And forgive us our debts, as we forgive our debtors.**
> **¹³ And lead us not into temptation, but deliver us from evil. For the kingdom is Yours and the power and the glory forever. Amen."**

Jesus gave us an outline on how to pray. He does not want

us to repeat this prayer every time we pray. Once we understand what each phrase means, we can effectively enter the throne room of grace and petition our Father according to His will. As we are examining each phrase, also note the particular order the prayer is in, as there is a reason for this.

"Our Father who is in heaven, Holy is your name." – Jesus is telling us to start every prayer with praise to the Father. Most think the first logical thing to do is ask Him to forgive us our sins, but that is further down the list.

> "Come into His gates with gifts of thanks, and into His courts with praise. Praise Him and adore His name." – Psalm 100:4

As the Psalmist states, when we come in through His gates and enter the very place where He abides, we should bring gifts of thanks, praise and adoration for His name. We should let Him know how Majestic, Magnificent, Holy, Righteous, True, Merciful, Gracious, and just how Awesome He is. Let Him know how worthy He is to be praised by His creation.

By spending a large portion of our opening prayer praising our heavenly Father, He is more receptive to hearing the rest of our prayer. So, what you are saying is we should butter Him up so He will give us what we ask for later? God forbid! God knows the difference between a heartfelt praise from His children than a schmoozing car salesmen trying to sell Him on something. You can't con God.

Unlike others, He knows the heart.

God is more receptive to hearing our prayers when we start out by praising and worshipping Him because His ear hears someone who is truly thankful for Him and who He is, not someone who starts out just wanting something from Him.

In Luke 17:11-19, the bible tells a story about Jesus healing ten lepers. After he healed them, He told them to go and present themselves to the priest, as was required by the law. On the way, one of the ten realized what Jesus had done for Him and went back and fell on his face at Jesus' feet and with a very loud voice praised God for what He had done. Jesus said, "Were there not ten lepers cleansed? Where are the other nine? None of them returned to give God glory except this stranger."

Do you wonder why this event made it into Luke's gospel account of Jesus' life? It's because when someone comes, with a very loud voice praising God, such thankfulness, love and devotion moves God. Your voice will drown out a million self-righteous prayers by approaching God in this manner. I know this from experience, I can testify to its truth. Praise and thankfulness moves God to act on your behalf because of your faith and gratitude towards Him.

"Your kingdom come" – What is the kingdom? The kingdom is what God will establish here on earth and where He currently abides, thus it is called the Kingdom of "God", as referenced in Luke 17:21; Luke 18:25-26; Luke

19:11; Luke 21:31; Mark 12:29-34; Matthew 21:31, 43-44. Only in the book of Matthew is the term "Kingdom of Heaven" (Matthew 18:1-9) used. I believe the New Bible Dictionary explains very well why two different terms to explain the same place was used.

[1]"KINGDOM OF GOD, KINGDOM OF HEAVEN. The kingdom of heaven or kingdom of God is the central theme of Jesus' preaching, according to the Synoptic Gospels. While Matthew, who addresses himself to the Jews, speaks for the most part of the 'kingdom of heaven', Mark and Luke speak of the 'kingdom of God', which has the same meaning as the 'kingdom of heaven', but was more intelligible to non-Jews. The use of 'kingdom of heaven' in Matthew is certainly due to the tendency in Judaism to avoid the direct use of the name of God. In any case no distinction in sense is to be assumed between the two expressions (cf., e.g., Mt. 5:3 with Lk. 6:20)."

After the "Great White Throne Judgment", this earth will be totally destroyed and a new heaven (the sky we see) and a new earth will be created. It is there that God's kingdom will forever be. It will be as God intended in the Garden of Eden. There will be no sin, no tears, no pain, no sorrow, no worry, no stress, no work and no death. We will live in the

---

[1] Wood, D. R. W., & Marshall, I. H. (1996). New Bible dictionary (3rd ed.) (647). Leicester, England; Downers Grove, IL: InterVarsity Press.

kingdom with God as the Supreme Ruler. There will be no night nor a sun to light our days because the brightness of God's glory will be our light. (Revelation 22:5)

Verse 33 of this chapter states we should seek His kingdom.

> "But seek the kingdom of God and His righteousness first, then all these things will be provided for you." – Matthew 6:33

We are a traveler in this world in search of another kingdom, a kingdom where God dwells.

"Your will be done, on earth as it is in heaven" – Jesus teaches us the importance of praying for God's will when we pray. Our will is not His, and we do not always know His will in every given situation.

We can pray for someone to be healed, but it might be His will for the person to die with that particular illness. We do not know when a person's time on earth is done, only God knows that. Therefore, we should always pray for God's will.

> "Come now, you that say, "Today or tomorrow we will go into a certain city and stay there a year, to buy and sell, and make a profit:" whereas you do not know what tomorrow holds. For what is your life? Is it not but a vapor, that appears for a little time, and then vanishes away. For you should say, "If the Lord will, we will live and do this or that." –

James 4:13-15

Jesus instructs us to pray for God's will and James instructs us to acknowledge God's will. Jesus incorporated it into His prayer before His crucifixion when He prayed;

> "Saying, Father, if you are willing, remove this cup from Me: nevertheless, not My will but Yours be done." Luke 22:42

We can see from Jesus' own prayer life that He used the example He gave us. He was willing to deny Himself and what His flesh wanted in order for God's will to be done. There will be times when our will conflicts with God's will and that is when decision time comes. Do we succumb to our own will or do we unselfishly as Jesus did, pray for God's will to be done regardless of what we are wanting?

> "I delight to do your will O my God. Yes, your law is written in my heart." – Psalm 40:8

Our delight should be to do God's will. It is for this reason we should pray that God's will in heaven be the same here on earth in all of our lives.

"Give us this day our daily bread" – Notice it only deals with today, not yesterday or tomorrow, only today. This is in line with the closing verse for this chapter.

> "Do not worry about tomorrow, for tomorrow will worry about itself. Each day has its own difficulties." – Matthew 6:34

We are to pray for God to meet our needs of the day. Praying for future needs is not biblical, nor is praying for things we do not need. Have you been paying attention to the order of this prayer like I told you to in the beginning? Because here is where I connect the order of the prayer to show you something awesome.

- We started out with praise.
- We then prayed that His kingdom would come.
- We then ask Him to perform His will.
- Now, we are asking Him to meet our daily needs.

"But seek the kingdom of God and His righteousness first, then all these things will be provided for you." – Matthew 6:33

Yes, this verse shows up again. I want you to notice something in how Jesus has us praying here. We first praised God, then we sought His kingdom FIRST, then we prayed for His will, and finally we are asking Him to meet our daily needs. Jesus, in the Lord's Prayer, has us seeking the kingdom of God first and then asking for needs, thereby guaranteeing that we did things in the correct order for "all these things, as in our daily bread, being provided for us." Pardon the Southern English, but ain't that awesome? If you didn't catch that, then go back and re-read this paragraph again until you get it. The Holy Spirit actually pointed that out to me as I was writing this portion of the book. I had never really paid attention to the order of the prayer, nor did I ever connect the kingdom of God in the prayer to seeking the kingdom first. Nothing like getting a revelation of something yourself when trying to teach others. Sorry for getting all giddy on you, but I am pretty excited right now. God is so good.

"And forgive us our debts, as we forgive our debtors." –

[2]"Jesus often speaks about people being debtors to God (Mt. 6:12; 18:23ff.; Lk. 7:41; 17:10), but only in Mt. 6:12 is sin specifically equated with debt. Jesus uses the illustration of debt to explain the human situation vis-à-vis God. The debt is so great that no good deeds can offset it. We are totally dependent on the divine mercy."

The Greek word for debt is opheílēma (ὀφείλω). It literally means a debt or obligation. As one bible commentator put it;

> "As the debtor in the creditor's hand, so is the sinner in the hands of God." – Jamieson, Fausset, Brown

There was a certain king that was collecting debts that his servants owed him. One servant owed him 10,000 talents.

---

[2] Kittel, G., Friedrich, G., & Bromiley, G. W. (1985). Theological Dictionary of the New Testament (747). Grand Rapids, MI: W.B. Eerdmans.

Since the servant did not have the money to pay, the king ordered him, his wife, his children and all that he had to be sold and applied to the debt. The servant fell down before the king begging and said, "Give me just a little more time and I will pay all that I owe you." The king was moved with compassion and forgave the servant his entire debt.

The servant left and went to find a fellow servant that owed him 100 denarii. When he found him, he grabbed him by the throat and said, "Pay me all that you owe me now." The fellow servant fell down before him begging and said, "Give me just a little more time and I will pay you all that I owe you." He would not allow him anymore time and had him thrown into prison until he paid everything that was owed.

The other fellow servants, seeing what happened, went and told the king. The king was furious and sent for the servant. When the guards apprehended him, the king said, "I forgave you all your debt because you begged me, and you could not show the same mercy to your fellow servant?" The king then ordered the servant to be taken to the jailers and tortured until every last penny was paid.

That story that I just paraphrased was taken from Matthew 18:21-35. It demonstrates what God will do to us if we do not show the same compassion that He shows us. He forgives us our debt, so we should in return show the same mercy and forgive those who sin against us. This includes everyone who has talked bad about us, made us angry, and cheated us, stole from us, committed adultery with our spouse and just about any other bad thing they have done to us. Failure to forgive others, regardless of how bad the crime against us, will result in God not forgiving us our sins.

"And lead us not into temptation, but deliver us from evil." – God does not tempt us.

> "Let no man say when he is tempted, "I am tempted by God": for God cannot be tempted with evil, nor does He Himself tempt any man,"" – James 1:13

There are two ways temptation takes place. One is by our own lust.

> "but every man is tempted, when he is dragged away by his own lust and enticed to sin." – James 1:14

The other way is by the Holy Spirit's leading. Though He does not tempt us, He can lead us to the place, as He did Job, Abraham and Jesus, where Satan tempts us.

> "Then Jesus was led into the wilderness by the Spirit to be tempted by the devil." – Matthew 4:1

This builds faith in Christ, teaches us how to engage in spiritual warfare and makes us stronger to face even tougher challenges in our lives. But we do not have to worry about the temptation being too much for us, for God will not allow any more than we can bare.

> "There is no temptation that has overtaken you except that which belongs to man; and God is trustworthy, who will not allow you to be tempted above what you are able *to withstand*, but will with every temptation also make a way for you to escape, that you may be able to endure it." – 1 Corinthians 10:13

God always makes a way to escape the temptation. An exit strategy has already been implemented. It is God saying, "STOP, my child has had enough!", and the devil stops. We just have to have faith in God that He is in full control.

So, what does "Lead us not into temptation" really mean? Asking that question of Scholars and Bible Commentators will get you so many different answers it will leave you more confused that when you first started studying.

> ""God, while he does not 'tempt' men to do evil (James 1:13), does allow his children to pass through periods of testing. But disciples, aware of their weakness, should not desire such testing, and should pray to be spared exposure to such situations in which they are vulnerable." (R.T. France)

I believe that is one of the best answers I have found among Bible Commentators. We should pray to be spared from testing of which we are vulnerable, as we all have different vulnerabilities. Again, God does not tempt man, but He does allow and will sometimes lead us, as the

SERMON ON THE MOUNT: THE BELIEVER'S HANDBOOK

example of Jesus, to square off against the devil. It is those times of testing that we should pray that when we square off against the devil, it is not in an area of which we are vulnerable, thereby granting a victory besides a failure.

Some Scholars and Bible Commentators argue that by God leading us to a place to be tempted that is just the same as Him tempting us, to which I answer, "No it's not".

As God's children, we are fighters. We fight the good fight of faith. (1 Timothy 6:12) We are clothed from head to toe in our fighting armor. (Ephesians 6:11-17) Being the fighter's we are, God will sometimes setup a fight for us. Being the proud Father He is, He drives us to our bout against the devil. He remains there to make sure things do not get out of hand or the devil try to cheat us. We enter the ring, of which God has set the rules, and we square off against our enemy, the devil.

Now, there is a big difference in God driving us to the fight (leading us by His Spirit as He did Jesus), than Him driving us to the fight and then punching us in the face. He just drove us there, the devil is the one that punched us in the face. It is the devil that does the tempting, not God. I hope this fighting analogy shows the difference between being led somewhere and being tempted.

Now, let's carry this analogy a little further. Our Father knows we have a weak chin, as He is the one that trains us. While we are in the ring fighting the devil, we hope and pray God does not let Him hit us on the chin, which is where we are the most vulnerable. Now, do you see what the scripture means?

What is this vulnerability that you speak of? Each person has different weaknesses. One might have a problem with lust, one might have problems with porn, one might have a problem with alcohol, one might have a problem with gambling and the list goes on. You do not want God to drive you to a liquor store if you have a problem with alcohol. You do not want God to drive you to a casino if you have a gambling problem. By God allowing the devil to tempt you in those areas, He is allowing the devil to attack your weakness. Now, this is not always a bad thing. God will at times allow you to overcome your vulnerability in tiny temptations, building you up with each victory. I say "tiny temptations", because if He turned the devil loose on you with a full blown temptation, your weak flesh would most definitely give in.

"For the kingdom is Yours and the power and the glory forever. Amen." – And finally we end up like we started our prayer, giving thanks and praise to the One who deserves it most, our heavenly Father.

If we will follow this pattern for our prayers that Jesus has set, we will start to see a real change in the effectiveness or our prayer life. Many people approach prayer as something mystical, hard and burdensome to do. We should approach prayer as a natural conversation between a Father and a child.

I believe the hardest thing about prayer for most is the fact you are talking to someone you cannot see. We know that in just about any psychology book published, that we would be labeled as having some type of weird psychological disorder. What sane person talks to their imaginary friend? We left that in our childhood. No reasonable adult talks to someone they cannot see.

Whether consciously or subconsciously, that is pretty much what hinders us in our prayer life. First, God is not an imaginary friend. He is just as real as you and me. You know He is real because you feel His presence inside you. Second, we must know that when we talk to our "invisible" God, that He hears us and answers our prayers according to His will.

I often talk to God as if I was talking to someone sitting straight across from me. In plain ole Arkansas English to boot. I sometimes catch myself talking to Him in my holy voice. You know what I'm talking about. That real deep sincere humble voice you get when you pray, your holy voice. Where you no longer say Jesus naturally, you say it like this: Jeeezzzus. Sometimes I throw in some lip smacking too. ☺ I just laugh at myself and switch back to my regular voice, because God wants the real me, not a voice act that I put on just for Him. I talk to Him just as if He were visible. That is how you "pray". Forget that you are "praying" and then you can really start to communicate with God and build a relationship with Him.

¹⁴ For if you forgive men their offences, your heavenly Father will also forgive yours. ¹⁵ But if you do not forgive men their offences, neither will your Father forgive yours.

Forgiveness is mandatory. Those three words sum up what Jesus is teaching here. It brings to mind a Christian end times movie, can't recall the name, where a Christian is being tortured to get him to agree to work as a spy for the Antichrist. The man who was torturing him stated, "I just love torturing Christians, because the whole time you are torturing them, they are forgiving you." I laughed when he said it, but later thought on how true the statement should be.

The fruit of the Spirit that most associate with Christians is love. The second thing they should note about us is that we are very forgiving, which is really a product of the love of Christ in us.

> "And be kind to one another, tenderhearted, forgiving each other just as God in Christ forgave you." – Ephesians 4:32

The Apostle Paul exhorts us, just as Christ did, to be kind to one another, tenderhearted, and forgive each other, for God, because of what Christ accomplished on the cross, forgave us or our sins.

¹⁶ And when you fast, do not be like the hypocrites, with a sad gloomy face. For they disfigure their faces

so they may appear to men to be fasting. Truly, I say to you, they have been given their reward. ¹⁷ But you, when fasting, anoint your head and wash your face, ¹⁸ so that you may not appear to men to be fasting, but to your Father who is in secret. And your Father, who sees what you have done in secret, will openly reward you.

The following are scriptures related to fasting that you can look up in your Bible if you wish to further study fasting:

Exodus 34:28; Deuteronomy 9:9, 18; Judges 20:26; 1 Samuel 7:6, 31:13; 2 Samuel 1:12, 3:35, 12:16; 1 Kings 19:8, 21:27; 2 Chronicles 20:3; Ezra 8:21, 10:6; Nehemiah 1:4, 9:1; Esther 4:3, 16; Psalm 35:13, 69:10; Jeremiah 14:12, 36:9; Daniel 6:18, 9:3, 10:3; Joel 1:14; Zechariah 7:5, 8:19; Matthew 4:2, 9:14, 17:21; Mark 2:18, 9:29; Luke 2:37, 5:33, 18:12; Acts 13:2-3, 14:23, 27:9; 1 Corinthians 7:5; 2 Corinthians 6:5, 11:27

"And when you fast" – The first thing we notice is it is assumed that we will fast. It doesn't say "if you fast". So, how often should we fast? Unfortunately the bible does not tell us how often we should fast. That is something that God works out with each person individually.

Jesus said that if we have faith as a grain of a mustard seed, we can say to the mountain to be removed from its current place and placed elsewhere, and it will move. In the next verse though, He tells us that this kind of faith is only obtainable by prayer and fasting. (Matthew 17:20, 21)

So, there are things in our spiritual life that will only come by prayer and fasting. If we choose to have the kind of faith mentioned in Matthew 17, then we must fast.

This brings up the question, what do we fast from? Food? Water? Most all examples in the bible are from food and water. But what about those with an illness, such as diabetes, what can they fast from since missing a meal can be detrimental to their health? Or those who take medicine that require drinking lots of water, what can they fast from?

I would recommend fasting from coffee, cola, tea or other beverages than water if you require the liquids. For most, giving up cola, coffee or tea is worse than giving up water which a lot of us doesn't even drink anyway. As far as food, if you can't miss a meal for health reasons, I would recommend giving up your favorite snack or food that you eat regularly. Make sure it is something that you really crave and like that is eaten often.

The whole purpose behind fasting is to deny the flesh and bring it under subjection to God. The flesh craves things, it has addictions and to deny it the pleasures it seeks makes it submit to the things of the Spirit. How often you fast is up to you and God. If you seek a close relationship with Christ and desire those spiritual things that only prayer and fasting can bring, then fasting must be part of your life.

The only rule that Jesus explicitly gave us on fasting is not to be like the hypocrites, who have depressed looks so people know something is going on with them. They do this so people will inquire about what is wrong so they can say, "Oh nothing, I am just fasting and …" They want the glory of man and to look spiritual in other people's eyes.

We should be very, I mean very, discreet when we fast. We should pick a time when we can be alone with God and nobody will know we are fasting. We do not have to fast 40 days, unless of course God told us to. We can fast a meal a day for five days or a meal a day for a couple of days, or just one meal. It doesn't matter when we fast if it is a time when others are not privy to the fact we are fasting. That is why splitting our fast up into several days of one meal usually works best, or several days straight through of not drinking cola, coffee or tea.

Study all the other scriptures I listed at the beginning and pray about what the Lord would want you to do. Fasting is personal and tailored to the individual. The only exception is if your Church declares a fast, that is the only instance of others knowing you are fasting, and even then it should be done privately, not making an issue of the fact you are fasting.

19 Do not store up treasures on earth for yourselves, where the moth and rust destroy them and where thieves break in and steal them. 20 But store up treasures in heaven for yourselves, where neither the moth nor rust destroys, and where thieves do not break in and steal them. 21 For where your treasure is, your heart will be there also.

The key verse to these passages is twenty-one. "For where your treasure is, you heart will be there also." What a man loves, he gives his heart to, and he gives it his all, his full focus and attention. It is what his mind continually stays on. It rules his day and his dreams at night.

This same kind of passion is shown toward money or worldly wealth, our earthly treasure. Men seek it, steal it, and kill for it, and lie and cheat to get it. It is what gives man power and fame. It attracts the opposite sex, so it gives man a false love, attention and affection. This is the type of treasure one should not make the object of his affection, yet our televisions, radios and churches are full of preachers teaching us to "plant a seed and reap a harvest", or "speak positive and our words will produce wealth", or "name it and claim it".

> "To the elders who are among you, I exhort as a fellow elder, and as a witness to the sufferings of *Jesus* Christ, and as a partaker of the glory that will be revealed. Shepherd the flock of God that is among you, taking care of them, not under obligation, but willingly; not for greediness or material gain, but eagerly;" – 1 Peter 5:1-2

Our Pastors are instructed to willingly and eagerly serve the flock, not because they are greedy or want material gain, but because they want to fulfill the calling of God on their life and be a servant to God's people. But this is not what we see in our Pastors today, and it is an end time fulfillment of scripture.

> "And through greediness with fabricated words their business will be to exploit you: whose judgment of long ago is not idle, and their destruction is not asleep." – 2 Peter 2:3

In Peter's second letter, he tells how these preacher's will make it their business to exploit you with their fabricated stories. In order to get your wealth, they must preach a gospel of wealth that tickles your ears and excites your greed. It's one of the oldest cons in the book. Convince someone that can give a little and get a lot, or if they give a lot they will get an overflow of wealth. They teach you must desire this wealth with your whole heart because it is only when you desire something with your whole heart that God answers your prayer. They are teaching you to lay up your treasures on earth and to seek worldly things, which is totally contrary to the word of God. The bible says you can't love God and worldly wealth. (Matthew 6:24)

Where your heart is, there is your treasure. Our treasure should be God and doing His will. Our entire being, our hearts desire, our deepest craving from within should be focused totally upon Him. It is only then we truly seek heavenly treasure.

So how do we get this heavenly treasure? Jesus instructed a man to go sell all that he had, give it to the poor and he would have treasure in heaven. (Matthew 19:21) Jesus knew the man was very attached to his possessions and would not comply with His instructions. But Jesus did show us that by righteous acts we store treasure in heaven.

If we help the poor, lead a person to Christ, support a missionary, feed the hungry, etc. we are laying up treasure in heaven. But, we must follow the guidelines Jesus has set in these three chapters on doing these righteous act, such as keeping them secret, etc. If our heart is into doing these things, then our treasure will surely be in heaven, where one day we will collect our reward from Christ.

22 The lamp of the body is the eye. Therefore, if the eye is healthy, your whole body shall be full of light. 23 But if your eye is wicked, your whole body will be full of darkness. Therefore, if the light that is in you is darkness, how great that darkness is!

To best explain this, let's look at a couple other commentators besides myself.

> "Wealth not only enslaves the heart, but it also enslaves the mind (Matt. 6:22, 23). God's Word often uses the eye to represent the attitudes of the mind. If the eye is properly focused on the light, the body can function properly in its movements. But if the eye is out of focus and seeing double, it results in unsteady movements. It is most difficult to make progress while trying to look in two directions at the same time. If our aim in life is to get material gain, it will mean darkness within. But if our

outlook is to serve and glorify God, there will be light within. If what should be light is really darkness, then we are being controlled by darkness; and outlook determines outcome. (Wiersbe, W: Bible Exposition Commentary. 1989. Victor)

"The eye that is bad is the heart that is selfishly indulgent. The person who is materialistic and greedy is spiritually blind. Because he has no way of recognizing true light, he thinks he has light when he does not. What is thought to be light is therefore really darkness, and because of the self-deception, how great is the darkness! The principle is simple and sobering: the way we look at and use our money is a sure barometer of our spiritual condition. (MacArthur, J: Matthew 1-7 Macarthur New Testament Commentary Chicago: Moody Press)"

We can see from the two commentators that Jesus is preparing us for the next verse (24) by explaining to us the spiritual condition of our heart by using the eye as an example. So let's look at the next verse which deals with the very heart of greed and the hold that riches can have on us.

24 No one can serve two Lords. He will either hate the one or love the other, or else he will cling to the one and despise the other. You cannot serve God and worldly wealth.

Money is an idol waiting to happen, because it promises everything that is good here on earth. If you have worldly wealth, you can purchase whatever you like on whim. It brings you social status among the most revered people on earth. Yes, you can rub elbows with the rich and famous and having them coveting all that you have, giving you a sense of pride and accomplishment. In order to keep this status, your lust and thirst for more will never cease.

If you have great wealth, it is almost impossible not to make it your God and it be your Master. Now note I said, "Almost" impossible, so don't go off saying I said all rich people are going to burn like a dead oak branch in the fires of hell. But I will venture to say that it will probably be less than .05% that can have great wealth and keep their heart focused on God. Let's look at some other scriptures on money.

> "For the love of money is the root of every kind of evil: which while some striving to obtain it have been led away from the faith, and have pierced themselves with much grief." – 1 Timothy 6:10

At the root of every kind of evil is money. You probably cannot name one preacher that once he becomes nationally known and on television or his ministry grows large, doesn't start to focus on money. He continually pumps out one book after another, one music cd after another, one teaching DVD after another and the current is more life changing than the previous.

Most large ministries hire staff writers that write the majority of their commentaries, bibles and books and the Minister or Ministries name gets put on it, without writing a single word. It is because one person cannot produce that much product and the money will soon dry up if they do not keep a constant flow of new product. What is worse is when they make their commercial to sell you their new product, they lead you to believe they were the ones that wrote the books or commentaries. This is blatant deception and outright lying. This is the exact thing 2 Peter 2:3 was talking about when he stated that with feigned words their "business would be to exploit you" because of their greed. We can expect this kind of evil from the world, but from a so-called professing believer, it should never once be named among us.

> "Now he who sowed seed among the thorn bushes is the one who hears the word, and due to the cares of this world and the pleasure of riches the word is choked, and he becomes unfruitful." – Matthew 13:22

That scripture explains beautifully why once a preacher becomes nationally known and successful his heart is fixed on money. It's because the "pleasure of riches" and the anxiety associated with such choke the word. My intension is not to just nitpick preachers, as the same applies to successful Christian businessmen also. As their business grows and they are more in demand with travel, meetings, etc., their spiritual life goes into a downhill spiral that is out of control. In their pursuit to build a bigger empire, the word is choked and they too become unfruitful.

Let me give you a real example of a man that was on fire for God, whom God used to do numerous miracles, such as raising the dead, the lame walking, etc. This man that I speak of is Smith Wigglesworth, who lived from the mid 1800's to the early 1900's. He would leave a legacy that most men of God would love to have. The following is a paragraph from the book: "Wigglesworth: The Complete Story, by Julian Wilson, pg. 26"

"One year during the mid-1880s, severe winter weather gripped Bradford and Wigglesworth and his two employees were inundated with calls to repair burst water pipes. Such was the havoc wreaked by the storms and freezing conditions during that winter that he was kept busy for the next two years repairing the damage. To keep up with the work, he started missing mid-week and Sunday services at the mission and devoted little time to prayer and Bible study, with the inevitable result that his relationship with God began to suffer. As his faith cooled, Polly, now burdened with pastoring the church alone, became more fervent. And as her zeal contrasted starkly with his spiritual indifference, it began to irritate him intensely. His innate weaknesses – his volcanic temper, impatience and tactlessness – previously held at bay by godly self-control, became more pronounced. Irritable and taciturn, he became critical and difficult to please. Polly's refusal to be provoked and retaliate only incensed him more until matters came to a head one night."

That is an example of a man that God greatly used who let the cares of this life gradually lead him away and eventually lose his relationship with God in the process. He quit his job as a plumber after realizing that he had backslid and went full time working for God. He lived many more years and would eventually come to America and leave his mark here also.

We cannot pursue wealth here on earth and please God, regardless of what your modern, seeker friendly Pastor may tell you. A roof over your head, food on your table and Jesus in your heart is all you need here on earth. Anything else just complicates your life. We cannot love God and worldly wealth.

Jesus didn't have wealth, the Apostles didn't have wealth, the early church were mostly poor people, but they had great riches. We do read in Revelation about one church that did have wealth but was very poor.

> "17 Because you say, I am rich and prosperous and have need of nothing: and do not know that you are wretched, miserable, poor, blind and naked, 18 I advise you to buy from Me gold purified by the fire, that you may be rich; and white garments, that you may be clothed, that the shame of your nakedness is not shown; and anoint your eyes with salve, so that you may see." Revelation 3:17-18

This is the condition of the Church today in America. It is prosperous and rich but cannot see that it is really wretched, miserable, poor, blind and naked. We have put our trust in riches and the pursuit of worldly things, forsaking the things of God. Let us seek your kingdom and righteousness Father, knowing that all of our needs will be met by your divine grace and love.

25 This is why I say to you, "Do not worry about your life, what you will eat or what you will drink. Nor for your body, what you will wear. Is not life more than food and the body more than clothing? 26 Look at the birds of the air, they do not sow, nor do they reap, nor gather into barns, yet your heavenly Father feeds them. Are you not much more valuable than they? 27 Which of you by being anxious can add one foot to his height?

> "Not that I speak in regard to being in need: for I have learned, in whatever state I am in, to be content. I know how to be brought low by poverty, and I know how to live in abundance: everywhere and in all things I have learned to both be full and to be hungry, both of having abundance and suffering need." – Philippians 4:11-12

The Apostle Paul learned that whatever state he found himself in, to be content. To be content is to be satisfied. If you are satisfied, you do not go seeking something more than what you currently have. But most of us are not satisfied living paycheck-to-paycheck. We want more than that. Most of us are not satisfied with several thousand in the bank, a car for each family member and whatever we want to eat on the table. We want more than that. Most of us are not satisfied with a thriving business making a few million per year. We need to triple profits next year. Yes, again, we want more.

Have you noticed that regardless where we are in life, from poor, middle class to rich, no class is ever satisfied? That is because satisfaction does not come from worldly things. We will never be satisfied if we are depending on worldly things to make us happy.

Jesus is telling us to not worry about those things, what we will eat or drink. He gives us an example of the birds being able to eat and they don't even work, yet God takes care of them. He then says, "Are you not more valuable than them?" We shouldn't concern ourselves with what we will eat or drink, because our heavenly Father loves us so much He will always provide for our needs.

28 And why are you worried about clothes? Closely observe the lilies of the field and how they grow. They do not work, nor do they spin. 29 But I say to you, that even Solomon in all his glory was not clothed like one of these. 30 Therefore, if God so clothed the grass of the field, which exist today and tomorrow is thrown into the furnace, shall He not much more clothe you? O you of little faith! 31

Therefore, do not be anxious, saying, "What shall we eat?" or "What shall we drink?" or "What shall we wear?" 32 For the heathen seek after all these things, and your heavenly Father knows that you need all these things. 33 But seek the kingdom of God and His righteousness first, then all these things will be provided for you.

"Do not be anxious, saying, "What shall we eat?" or "What shall we drink?" because it is the sinner who seeks after such things.

No, Jesus didn't make a mistake when He said it was the sinner that sought after worldly things. He teaches us that if we seek first the kingdom of God and His righteousness, then God will give us all these things. In other words, put God first in all that we do and He will provide all our physical needs, and that is a promise. We should concern ourselves with the things of God, not with what is here on earth. God knows we have to have food, shelter and clothing and He will make sure we have all of that without even asking Him for it.

What God is not promising is great riches. He will provide the necessities to sustain life in this fleshly body, and with that, as with the Apostle Paul, we should be content.

34 Do not worry about tomorrow, for tomorrow will worry about itself. Each day has its own difficulties.

God is not saying we cannot plan for the future, but we

should not worry about what will happen tomorrow or next year. And as we are planning for the future, we should do so with this in mind:

> "Come now, you that say, "Today or tomorrow we will go into a certain city and stay there a year, to buy and sell, and make a profit:" whereas you do not know what tomorrow holds. For what is your life? Is it not but a vapor, that appears for a little time, and then vanishes away. For you should say, **"If the Lord will, we will live and do this or that**." – James 4:13-15

We should always say, "If the Lord will" we will do this or we will do that. In one little second our whole world can change. In a moments time we can lose a loved one or even die ourselves. We do not know what God has in store for us even a second from now. As the old saying goes and forever holds true, "The things we worry about most never happen."

Jesus teaches us not to worry. Why? Because He has everything under control. God will provide our needs so all we need to concern ourselves with is serving Him. What Master doesn't provide food, clothing and shelter for his servants? Anybody that has watched a western knows the ranch hand gets his meals, clothing and a bunkhouse to sleep in, is God not so much better than that? That is a modern day parable. ☺

CHAPTER 7

¹ Do not judge, so you are not judged. ² For the verdict you pass on another will be used to judge you. And with the measure you give out, you will receive the same measure in return. ³ And why do you see the splinter that is in your brother's eye, but do not notice the log that is in your own? ⁴ Or how can you say to your brother, "Let me pull the splinter out of your eye" and look, a log is in your own eye? ⁵ You hypocrite, first take the log out of your own eye, and then you can see clearly to take the splinter out of your brother's eye.

Matthew 7:1 is the verse out of the bible that every sinner knows and draws like a switchblade. Matthew 7:1 is the verse that every Christian knows and draws like a switchblade. But both groups rarely have a clue what it even means.

First thing to note, IT DOES NOT mean to not judge. Someone who does not judge (or have discernment basically is what judge means) will be lead away by every silly doctrine the devil and man can create. Jesus is teaching you how to judge, He is not telling you not to judge. And before you go all Pharisee on me, let me explain.

How can you say to your brother, you hypocrite, you gossip about everybody when you are gossiping about others yourself? You can't can you? But now, if you do not gossip, you can see clearly to correct the fault that your brother has. That is what Jesus means when He states, "take the log out of your own eye, and then you can see clearly to take the splinter out of your brother's eye." Did you notice He said that once the "log" is out of your eye, THEN you can SEE CLEARLY to take the SPLINTER out of your brother's eye?

As long as we are bogged down with the same faults, we can't correct others. Jesus is teaching you how to judge here, because later on in this chapter, He is going to have you judging. But first, let's look at some other scriptures on judging.

> "Do not judge according to appearance, but judge with righteous judgment." – John 7:24

> "But the spiritual man judges all things, yet he is judged by no one." – 1 Corinthians 2:15

> "For what have I to do with judging outsiders? Do you not judge those that are inside *the church*? But those outside *the church* God will judge. Therefore, remove those among you who are wicked." – 1 Corinthians 5:12-13

> "Beloved, do not believe every spirit, but try the spirits to see whether they are of God: because many false prophets have gone out into the world." – 1 John 4:1

Paul, to the Corinthians, plainly tells them that we judge those that are inside the church and instructed them to remove those that are wicked from the congregation. John, tells us to try the spirit to see if it's from God. This requires a judgment (or discernment) call in order to do so. Jesus is teaching us how to judge so we do not judge hypocritically and get ourselves in trouble with God.

One thing we do not do is judge the person's heart, for only God knows what is inside a man's heart. But his actions, his speech and the way he lives his life we are to judge, and this is solely for our own protection.

For instance, Mr. Happy Smiley Pastor that uses almost zero word of God and just wants us all to feel good because the world keeps us beat down will lead you straight to hell. Yes, we have to judge or we will follow blindly right through that broad gate to hell.

Oh, I almost forgot, "If we love Jesus, we keep His _____'s." If we do not keep His _____'s we do not love Him.

So, heed Jesus' word's here and do not judge hypocritically or you will receive the same judgment from God. Again, if you are caught up in the same fault you are judging, you are a hypocrite and will receive the same judgment in return.

I hate to bring up past sins of anyone, but it serves as the perfect example of hypocritical judging and I am only using it to illustrate this to you.

The following concerns Jimmy Swaggart and is taken from [3]Wikipedia.

"Swaggart's exposure came as retaliation for an incident in 1986 when Swaggart exposed fellow Assemblies of God minister Marvin Gorman, who had been accused of having several affairs. Once exposed, Gorman was defrocked from the Assemblies of God, his ministry all but ended. As a retaliatory move, Gorman hired his son Randy and son-in-law Garland Bilbo to stake out the Travel Inn on Airline Highway in New Orleans. A camera with a telephoto lens was placed in the window of the motel's Room 12 and draped with a black cloth. When Swaggart arrived, he reportedly went into Room 7. Randy Gorman and Garland Bilbo proceeded to let the air out of Swaggart's tires and called Marvin Gorman, whose church was located nearby. The two had taken photos of Swaggart outside of Room 7 with Debra Murphree, a local prostitute. Gorman showed up at the Travel Inn a short while later and asked Swaggart what he was doing there.

According to, Swaggart: The Unauthorized Biography of an American Evangelist by Ann Rowe Seaman, Gorman secured a promise from Swaggart that he would publicly apologize to Gorman and start the process of Gorman's reinstatement to the Assemblies of God. Gorman offered to remain silent if Swaggart would state publicly that he

---

[3] http://en.wikipedia.org/wiki/Jimmy_Swaggart

lied about Gorman's affairs. Gorman waited almost a year, then hand delivered a note to Swaggart informing him his time was up, but Swaggart did not respond. On February 16, 1988, Gorman contacted James Hamil, one of the 13-man Executive Presbytery of the Assemblies of God. Hamill in turn called Raymond Carlson, the Assemblies Superintendent. He summoned Hamill and Gorman to fly to Springfield and arranged for an emergency meeting of the presbyters. Carlson was shown photos of several men coming in and going out of Room 7 at the Travel Inn Motel in New Orleans. This was done in order to establish the fact that the room was being used for prostitution. One of the men seen leaving Room 7 was Jimmy Swaggart. The presbytery leadership of the Assemblies of God decided that Swaggart should be suspended from broadcasting his television program for three months."

Jimmy Swaggart had a fellow minister in the same organization who was having affairs kicked out of the Assemblies of God when he himself was having an affair with a prostitute. This is hypocritical at its core. Jimmy Swaggart admitted his sin and has put it all behind him and now has a successful television, bible and commentary business. I do not judge his heart or his commitment to Christ now. I agree with most of what he teaches and pray that his fall will be used for God's glory, just as David's in the bible. But let brother Swaggart's fall serve as an example to you that what Jesus said will happen. "If you judge hypocritically, you will receive the same judgment."

⁶ Do not give that which is holy to the dogs, and do not throw your pearls before swine, so they do not trample them under their feet, and then turn around and tear you to pieces.

At first glance this scripture doesn't make much sense, or at least it didn't to me for quite a while. But then again, I never quite understood Dr. Seuss' Green Eggs and Ham either.

"Don't give that which is holy" – What is holy? It would be the word of God.

"Do not throw your pearls before swine" – And what does the pearl represent? Wisdom and knowledge of course.

We are not to recklessly throw the word of God to those who are not willing to receive it. Jesus just gave us a good lesson on judging (or what some call discernment) and now He is going to make us use what He taught us. If we perceive that a person is not going to receive the word of God, we are not to present it to them. Let me give you an example.

A certain man, who I will not name, went on an Atheist talk show and every time he quoted any of the bible, they tore it to pieces and made fun of him. He did what this scripture is telling us not to do. He, knowing that they would mock the word of God and was not willing to change their views, kept giving them more scripture to attack and make fun of. We are not to present the holy word of God and the precious wisdom God has given us concerning His word to those who are unappreciative of it. In fact, Jesus told us to dust our feet off and move on when people didn't receive the word. (Matthew 10:14)

⁷ Ask, and it will be given to you; seek, and you will find; knock, and it will be opened to you. ⁸ For everyone who asks receives; and he that seeks finds; and to him that knocks it will be opened. ⁹ Or what man is there among you, who, if his son ask for a loaf of bread, would give him a stone? ¹⁰ Or, if he ask for a fish, would he give him a snake? ¹¹ If you, being wicked, know how to give good gifts to your children, how much more will your Father, who is in heaven, give good gifts to them that ask Him?

Once again, Jesus is teaching on the kindness and goodness of the Father. If we ask Him for our basic necessities, will He deny us? God forbid! He is a good Father who gives good gifts.

The asking, seeking and knocking does not only pertain to our worldly needs, but much more to our spiritual.

> "If any of you lack wisdom, let him ask God who gives to all men generously and without reproach; and it will be given to him. But let him ask in faith, without doubting, for he that doubts is like the wave of the sea, moved around and blown about by the wind. For that man should not think that he

will receive anything from the Lord." – James 1:5-8

But let us ask in faith, without doubting. God wants us to trust Him. If He said He will do it, consider it done, for God is faithful, trustworthy, and you can take it to the bank if He said it. We do not view spiritual things with our physical eyes. We view spiritual things with our spiritual eyes and physical things with our physical eyes, but what we see with our physical eyes does not dictate what is really happening spiritually. I hope I explained that where you understand. I probably made it sound more complicated than it is, so let's go with an example.

When I was a young evangelist, like seventeen years old young, my mother always drove me to the meetings and supported me in whatever I did. God has blessed me with an awesome mother who has always taken an active part in whatever I have done. Anyway, back to the story. I was scheduled to preach the morning and the evening service and we only had enough money to eat one meal that day, so we decided on breakfast.

When we arrived, we drove around the town and found a small country café to eat breakfast at, knowing by experience that small country café's always serve an awesome breakfast. We ordered our meal and while waiting on it to arrive, a woman sitting at the table beside us struck up a conversation and asked if I was a preacher. I guess it showed or something. ☺ She proceeded to tell us about the problems her daughter was having and I prayed for her while we were waiting on our food. When our food arrived, the lady excused herself, thanked us for praying for her daughter and left.

My mother and I enjoyed our great breakfast and sit and fellowshipped with each other awhile while killing time waiting for church to start. When it came time to leave, we take the check to the counter prepared to pay for our only meal of the day. The lady at the register informed us that we didn't owe anything for the meal, and of course, we asked why? She informed us that the lady sitting beside us paid for our meal when she paid for hers, leaving us with the money to buy a second meal that day.

In plain ole Arkansas English, "Now ain't God good?" Yes He is and He only gets gooder and gooder as time goes by. I was content with only eating one meal and never gave it a second thought, but oh did my heavenly Father ever give it thought. As I was seeking His righteousness and kingdom first, He was busy taking care of my physical needs, just like He promised He would. You see, I learned a long time ago that food and clothing is the least of my worries because God will always provide for me. That is the message Jesus is trying so hard to teach us here.

Spend your time serving God and do not even give it a thought of He will provide for you and your family, because I will stake my life on the fact that my God never fails. I might not always have what I want to eat, but He makes sure I eat. If what I have He considers appropriate for the day, who am I to question Him. I am thankful for whatever He chooses to provide for the day, and I can tell you right now, He has always provided more than enough. I am His child and He is never late on child support. ☺

12 Therefore, whatever you desire that men would do to you, do likewise to them: for this is the Law and the Prophets.

You learned this principle in kindergarten. Treat others like you want to be treated. Don't pull their hair, poke them in the eyes, bite them, and whatever you do, do not steal their woman or their ride. Not much needs to be said here.

If you really need more, then follow the "Hillbilly 10 Commandments". I could not find the author anywhere to give credit, but I am not the author of this.

1. Ain't but One God.
2. Honor yer Maw and yer Paw.
3. No tellin' tales or gossipin'.
4. Get yer hide ta Sunday meetin'.
5. Ain't nutin' comes before the Lord.
6. No foolin' with anuther feller's gal.
7. No killin', sept for critters.
8. Quit yer foul mouthin'.
9. No swipin' yer kinfolks stuff.
10. Don't be hankerin' fer it neither.

13 Enter in through the narrow door; for the door is wide and the road is spacious that leads to

destruction, and there are many that enter through it. [14] For the door is narrow and the road is difficult which leads to life, and there are few who find it.

The reason the door is narrow and the road difficult is because few, and I mean few even attempt to live by the principles that Jesus laid out for us in this three chapter sermon. Believing in Christ is just the beginning. We are saved by faith alone and not by our works, but if works do not follow, as in keeping Christ's commandments, salvation was never received. It is not, "I believe in Christ, now it's a free ride", because:

> "You believe there is one God; you do well: the devils also believe and are extremely afraid. Do you desire to know, O foolish man, that faith without works is dead?" – James 2:19-20

What James is saying is, "Salvation is by faith alone, but faith without works equals dead salvation, or no salvation at all." Just believing is not enough because even Satan and the demons believe in Jesus. We must follow His commandments He has given us. It is time for it again, are you ready?

If you love Jesus, you will keep His _____'s. If you do not keep His _____'s, you do not love Him. (John 14:15)

Here is the scriptural test to see if you know Jesus and are on the narrow road. I have saved this till the last of the book so it is fresh on your mind and one of the last things you will read.

> "And by this we know that we know Him, if we obey His commandments. He that says, "I know Him", and does not obey His commandments is a liar, and the truth is not in him. But whoever keeps His word, in him is the word of God completed: this is how we know we know Him. He that says he abides in Him should walk the same way He walked." – 1 John 2:3-6

The disciple, whom Jesus loved, preaches a different message than what we hear today. Jesus said if you love me, you will keep my commandments. John takes it a step further and says, "if you do not keep His commandment's, you are not saved and are a liar if you say you are." That is a pretty bold statement, don't you think? So, it is in our best interest to find out what His commandments are, huh?

So, how many Christians do you know that measure up to John's test to see if you are saved? Now do you see why that door is real narrow and the road travelling to it difficult? Living the Christ-like life is very hard to do.

Preacher's today have thrown out the baby with the bath water. They preach we are not under the law of Moses, which is 100% true, but they also teach we have complete freedom under Christ and able to do about anything we want, except we have to keep the ten commandments. But does the ten commandments tell you to turn the other cheek? No! Does the ten commandments tell you that if you insult your brother you could go to hell? No! You see, preachers have left out the entire law of Christ, His commandment's. And because of this, we have an entire generation of people who think they are saved and headed down the road to the narrow gate who are actually on the broad road to destruction.

I caution you brothers and sisters in Christ. Learn these three chapters by heart. Know what Christ expects of you. Read Matthew, Mark, Luke and John until you are sick of reading them and then read them some more. If you are not living the red, you are spiritually dead.

Jesus Teaches On Trees Bearing Fruit
(Luke 6:43-44)

15 Beware of false prophets who pretend to be good, but inside they are vicious wolves. 16 You will know them by their fruits. Do men gather grapes from a thorn-plant or figs from thistles? 17 In this manner every good tree produces good fruit; but a bad tree produces worthless fruit. 18 A good tree cannot produce worthless fruit, nor can a bad tree produce good fruit. 19 Every tree that does not produce good fruit is chopped down and cast into the fire. 20 Therefore, by their fruits you will know them.

As I stated at the start of this chapter, Jesus was teaching us how to judge so we do not judge hypocritically. For proper judgment, you must have discernment, which the Holy Spirit gives every believer that loves the truth of God's word. Here is another one of those times when we have to make a judgment call.

We will know a person by their fruit. It is impossible for an apple tree to produce an orange, likewise it is impossible for an orange tree to produce an apple. We can look at a person's life and tell whether they are of Christ or not. No matter how hard the wolf tries to act like the sheep, he will slip up and show some of his wolfieness (that is a word, I think) if we are watching.

Barnes, in his commentary on John 10:5 where Jesus said that His sheep will not follow a stranger, had this to say:

"This was literally true of a flock. Accustomed to the voice and presence of a kind shepherd, they would not regard the command of a stranger. It is also true spiritually. Jesus by this indicates that the true people of God will not follow false teachers - those who are proud, haughty, and self-seeking, as were the Pharisees. Many may follow such, but humble and devoted Christians seek those who have the mild and self-denying spirit of their Master ..."

Notice he said the "true people of God" would not follow a stranger, and of this I agree. We ultimately know Jesus by His word, what He has said to us and instructed us to do, just like a Shepherd of a flock. If we have read and studied His word, we will not listen to someone who is promising us that his oranges are really apples, because we know better.

If Mr. Happy Smiley False Prophet is not teaching you to follow the commandments of Christ, run as fast as you can in the opposite direction. Always a

pply the test of true discipleship that we studied in 1 John 2:3-6 when judging if someone is what they really claim to be. If their life does not reflect these three chapters, they are not following Christ. They are just deceiving their own selves, and possibly someone else in the process. Don't get mad at me, I am not the one who said it, the Apostle John did. And NO, there is not some other spiritual meaning to that passage.

21 Not everyone who says to me, "Lord", "Lord", will enter into the kingdom of heaven; but he who does the will of my Father who is in heaven. 22 Many will say to me on that day, "Lord", "Lord", did we not prophecy in your name? And in your name drive out demons? And in your name have we not done many mighty deeds? 23 And I will declare to them, "I never knew you; depart from me you who practice lawlessness."

These false believers thought what they had done was enough to save them, yet Jesus didn't even know them.

There is a golden gem of truth in this passage that if you grasp ahold of will change your spiritual life. Notice all these people claimed to do some pretty amazing things for Christ, such as prophecy, casting out demons and many might deeds. How did someone Christ didn't know do these things? I thought only Christians could do these things in the name of Jesus. Yeah, I thought wrong.

"Therefore, God has highly exalted Jesus, and given Him a name which is above every name: that at the name of Jesus every knee will bow, of those who are in heaven, and of those who are on earth, and of those under the earth; and every tongue will confess that Jesus Christ is Lord, to the glory of God the Father." – Philippians 2:9-11

Now don't be standing up reading this part because you might fall down. Don't be drinking anything or you might spit it on your neighbor. Here we go. God has highly exalted the name of Jesus. "Highly exalted!" His name is above every name. His name should not even be spoken without realizing the power in that name. We should not speak His name in jest, because all the evil powers in the heavens are frozen in fear and all the angels of heaven shout with praise every time that name is spoken. Every knee bows at that name. "EVERY KNEE". Come on now, get the revelation of this. It will change your life. Everything in heaven, everything on the earth and everything beneath the earth bows when that name is spoken. Visualize this in your mind. You speak His name and you see everything bowing, you see every tongue confessing that He is Lord, all for God to get the glory." Every demon, fallen angel and Satan himself is terrified of that precious name.

Here is the kicker, and this is why we see all of these people who have done these miracles using His name and not being known by Him. Take a long hard look at these names:

- Hebrew: Yeshua
- English: Jesus
- French: Jésus
- German: Jesus
- Swahilli: Jesus
- Arabic: Isa
- Greek: Ιησούς
- Chinese (Simplified Han): 耶稣
- Italian: Gesù
- Japanese: イエス・キリスト
- Korean: 예수
- Russian: Иисус
- Spanish: Jesús
- Bulgarian: Исус
- Czech: Ježíš
- Dutch: Jezus
- Estonian: Jeesus
- Haitian Creole: Jezi
- Hungarian: Jézus
- Romanian: Isus
- Thai: พระเยซู
- Turkish: Isa

When those names are spoken, even by a false prophet, the devil has to obey. In David Guzik's Bible Commentary concerning this verse, he states:

"Jesus did not seem to doubt their claims of doing the miraculous. He didn't say, "You didn't really prophesy or cast out demons or do miracles." This leads us to understand that sometimes miracles are granted through pretended believers, reminding us that in the final analysis, miracles prove nothing."

I agree with brother Guzik, but I don't even think He has the revelation of "they did it IN HIS NAME". What about the scripture that says, "How can Satan cast out Satan and his kingdom stand?" (Matthew 12:26) It isn't Satan that is casting out Satan, it is in obedience to the name of Jesus that the demons have to leave. It is in obedience to the name of Jesus that cancers are healed, even by false prophets. It is in obedience to the name of Jesus that the dead are raised, the lame walk, the blind see, and the deaf hear, even if being done by a false prophet. Are you getting it? It is the highly exalted, full of the Holy Ghost power, name of Jesus that is knocking the devil for a loop. Jesus himself tells us:

> "For many will come in my name, saying, "I am the Christ", and will lead many astray." – Matthew 24:5

Notice Jesus is not talking about false Messiah's here, for a false Messiah would not come in the name of Jesus, he would come in his own name, not another's. This is talking about false prophets coming in the name of Jesus and leading many people astray. How? By instantaneous miracles using the name of Jesus, the blind seeing, using His name, and the lame walking, using His name. You see, it is not only the believer that can use the name of Jesus and do miracles. Crazy isn't it? ☺

When a believer, or false believer, truly understands the authority and power in the name of Jesus, the only thing that can happen from then on is the miraculous. The name of Jesus can move a mountain from one place to another. Let's look at something awesome.

> "And when He had come to the other side, to the country of Gerasa, two demon possessed men met Him coming out of the tombs. They were so exceedingly violent that no one could pass by that way. And, behold, they cried out, saying, "What are you doing here Jesus, Son of God? Have you come to torment us before the time?" – Matthew 8:28-29

Those demons knew exactly who He was and what He is going to do to them when it's all said and done. Could Jesus have tormented them before the time? Sure He could, He is God. Those demons were mighty concerned that He had come there to do just that. That is the fear demons have when Jesus shows up, and just the mention of His name makes them tremble. Someone that comes in the authority of that name makes all heaven and earth tremble. Example time again.

I show up at your door with a warrant to search your property. It is signed by the judge. It is the judges name on that paper that gives me the authority to enter your home against your will. Without the judges name on that paper, I am powerless. But with his name, I can do everything he says I can on that search warrant. It doesn't matter if I know the judge or not, I have his name, and I came in his name. Are you getting it now? Oh man, my spirit just leaped inside me, literally, as I wrote this.

Do you see how the nonbeliever's did those miracles now? They had the judges name. Wow, that is such a powerful message to teach. I get all giddy inside.

Don't be fooled by miracles. Anyone who understands the power that the name of Jesus has can do them. I know that sounds crazy, even to me, but it is a fact that Jesus teaches. In order to know if someone is a true believer, you have to do the believer test of 1 John 2:3-6, are they keeping the commandments of Christ? A false prophet will not keep all these commandments, in fact, he will distort them.

24 Therefore, whoever hears My teachings and does them, I will compare him to a wise man who built his house upon a rock. 25 And the rain came down, and the floods came, and the winds blew and beat upon that house, but it did not fall, for its foundation was upon a rock. 26 And everyone who hears these words of Mine and does not do them, he will be compared to a stupid man who built his house on

the sand: ²⁷ And the rain came down, and the floods came, and the wind blew and beat upon that house, and it fell: and great was its fall.

Whoever hears the teachings of Jesus <u>and does them</u> is a wise man that builds his house on a very strong foundation. A foundation that is built on Jesus can withstand any storm that might come against it.

The Greek word mōrós means foolish or stupid. See, Jesus did talk like a southerner when He said a stupid man is the one who hears His words and doesn't do them. I think it's pretty stupid myself. He builds a foundation that isn't on our "rock" of salvation and when a storm comes the sand which isn't a solid foundation, and his house falls.

Jesus, in these three chapters, gave us a solid foundation to build our house on. If we are wise and not only hear His teachings, but do them also, then we are on the road to the narrow gate.

My friend, I beg of you to follow the teachings of Christ and write them upon your heart. Read these three chapters until you can almost quote them by heart. If you follow His teachings, you will be assured a place in His kingdom, that I pray comes quickly.

As I close, I leave you with one thing:

Those who love Jesus keep His _____'s. Those who do not keep His _____'s do not love Jesus. (John 14:15)

SERMON ON THE MOUNT: THE BELIEVER'S HANDBOOK

If you get anything out of this book, I hope it is to love Jesus and keep His commandments, even though they might be grievous to you, and even though you might lose some friends and family, prove your love by keeping His word.

28 And it came to pass when Jesus concluded these teachings, the people were amazed at His doctrine.

And I too, with the people that sat and listened to Jesus, am amazed at His doctrine. Jesus is so amazing and worthy of our praise. All glory and honor goes to Him, as we are nothing without Him.

TRIB NEW TESTAMENT PREVIEW

INTRODUCTION

The TRIB™ New Testament is a literal translation of the New Testament using the "New Testament in the Literal Greek: Byzantine Textform 2005" and the Textus Receptus. In translating the TRIB™ New Testament, both the religious and secular meanings were looked at in order to create the best possible translation of the words being dealt with. Many more resources were used from the Logos Bible Software System. I believe you will find the TRIB™ New Testament an easy to read literal translation that will find its place among other literal Byzantine translations, such as the King James Version (KJV), and the New King James Version (NKJV).

The TRIB™ translation can be used and quoted as "TRIB". Although it is a copy written work, I grant permission to quote in its entirety as long as the following copyright information is included:

©2012 TRIB™ New Testament. All Rights Reserved. Used by Permission.

Under no circumstance can the TRIB™ New Testament be sold. It must be available and offered for free. The electronic pdf version is free, with no requirements to purchase a paperback, leather bound or hardback cover copy. There is no difference between the .pdf files available and the book copy. The book copy will be available for those who prefer to have a book than read it electronically. Visit tribnewtestament.com for the .pdf files.

THE EPISTLE OF PAUL THE APOSTLE

TO THE

GALATIANS

CHAPTER 1

Greeting

1 Paul, an apostle, not from man, nor through man, but by Jesus Christ and God our Father, who raised Jesus from the dead; [2] and all the brothers who are with me, to the churches of Galatia:

[3] Grace and peace to you from God the Father, and from our Lord Jesus Christ, [4] who gave Himself for our sins, that He might rescue us from this present wicked age, according to the will of God our Father: [5] to whom be the glory forever and ever. Amen!

Do Not Listen To Any Other Gospel

[6] I am amazed that you have so soon turned your back on Him who called you into the grace of Christ to another gospel: [7] which is really not another; but there are some who trouble you, who want to change the gospel of Christ. [8] But though we, or a messenger from heaven, preach any other gospel to you, other than what we have preached, let him be cursed. [9] As we have already said, I will say it again, if anyone preaches any other gospel to you other than

what you have received from us, let him be cursed.

[10] For do I follow men, or God? Or do I seek the favor of men? For if I pleased men, I would not be the servant of Christ.

Paul's Apostleship Not from Man

[11] But I make known to you, brothers, that the gospel which was preached by me is not of man. [12] For I did not receive it from man, nor was I taught by man, it is the revelation of Jesus Christ.

[13] For you have heard of my conduct in the past while in Judaism, how I went overboard in persecuting the church of God and tried to destroy it: [14] and how I progressed in Judaism above many my age in the nation, being exceedingly zealous in the traditions of my fathers. [15] It pleased God, who set me apart while still inside my mother's womb, and called me by His grace, [16] to reveal Jesus in me, that I might preach Christ among the heathen; I did not immediately consult with other people: [17] nor did I go up to Jerusalem to those who were apostles before me, but I went to Arabia, and then returned to Damascus.

Paul Visits Peter in Jerusalem

[18] After three years, I went to Jerusalem to see Peter, and stayed with him for fifteen days. [19] I did not see any of the other apostles, except James, the Lord's brother. [20] The things which I write to you, before God, I do not lie. [21] Later I went to the districts of Syria and Cilicia. [22] The

churches of Judaea, which were in Christ, had never met me in person. ²³ But they had only heard, "He that formerly persecuted us now preaches the faith he once tried to destroy." ²⁴ And they praised God in me.

CHAPTER 2

Paul Defends the Gospel

2 After fourteen years, I went to Jerusalem again with Barnabas, and I also took Titus with me. ² And by revelation, I went and explained to them the gospel which I preach among the Gentiles, and privately to those of reputation, lest I run, or had run in vain. ³ And Titus, who was with me, being a Greek, was not compelled to be circumcised: ⁴ and that because of false brethren who, under false pretense joined us, to privately spy out our liberty which we have in Christ Jesus, that they may once again bring us into bondage; ⁵ to whom we did not yield submission, no, not even an hour; that the truth of the gospel might continue with you. ⁶ But of those who seemed to be something, (whoever they were, it makes no difference to me: God does not show partiality:) for those who seemed to be something added nothing to me: ⁷ On the contrary, when they saw that the gospel of the uncircumcision was given to me, as the gospel of the circumcision was to Peter; ⁸ (for He who works in Peter to the apostleship of the circumcision, the same was mighty in me toward the Gentiles:) ⁹ and when James, Peter and

John, who were thought to be leaders, perceived the grace that was given to me, they gave to me and Barnabas the right hands of fellowship; that we should go to the Gentiles, and they to the Jews. [10] The only thing they asked is that we remember the poor; of which, I was already eager to do.

Paul Scolds Peter for Hypocrisy

[11] But when Peter came to Antioch, I opposed him to his face, because he was to be blamed. [12] Before certain men came from James to Antioch, he ate with the Gentiles: but when they came, he stayed back and separated himself from the Gentiles, fearing them which were of the circumcision. [13] And the other Jews joined in with him; so much so that Barnabas was led astray with their hypocrisy. [14] But when I saw that they did not live according to the truth of the gospel, I said to Peter, before them all, "if you, being a Jew, live like the Gentiles, and not as the Jews do, then why do you compel the Gentiles to live like the Jews?"

[15] We who are Jews by nature, and not Gentile sinners. [16] Knowing that a man is not declared righteous by the works of the law, but by the faith of Jesus Christ, even we have believed in Jesus Christ, that we might be made righteous by the faith of Jesus Christ, not by the works of the law; for by the works of the law no man can be declared righteous. [17] But if, while we are trying to obtain righteousness by Christ, we ourselves are also found to be sinners, is Christ therefore the minister of sin? God forbid. [18] For if I rebuild

the things which I destroyed, I make myself a transgressor. [19] Through the Law, I died to the Law, that I might live to God. [20] I am crucified with Christ, yet I live; but it is not I that lives, but Christ that lives in me: and the life that I now live in this body, I live by the faith of the Son of God, who loved me and gave Himself for me. [21] I do not annul the grace of God: for if righteousness is by the law, then Christ died in vain.

CHAPTER 3

Righteousness through Faith

3 O foolish Galatians, who has bewitched you that you do not obey the truth, before whose eyes Jesus Christ was publicly portrayed among you as crucified? [2] This only would I ask of you, "Did you receive the Holy Spirit by the works of the law or by the hearing of faith?" [3] Are you so foolish? Having begun in the Spirit, are you now made complete by the flesh? [4] Have you suffered so much in vain? - if it indeed was in vain. [5] Therefore, he that ministers to you in the Spirit and works miracles among you, does he do it by the works of the law, or by the hearing of faith?

[6] Just as Abraham trusted in God and it was accounted to him as righteousness. [7] Therefore, know that those which are of faith, they are the sons of Abraham. [8] And the scripture, having previously known that God would justify

the Gentiles by faith, proclaimed in advance the gospel to Abraham, saying, "In you shall all nations be blessed." [9] So then they who are of faith are blessed with faithful Abraham.

[10] For those who trust in the works of the law are under a curse: for it is written, "Cursed is everyone who does not continue to do all things which are written in the book of the law." [11] But that no man is justified by the law in the sight of God is

evident: for, "The just shall live by faith." [12] For the law is not of faith: but, the man who does them shall live by them. [13] Christ has redeemed us from the curse of the law, having been made a curse for us: for it is written, "Cursed is everyone that hangs on a tree:" [14] that the blessing of Abraham might come upon the Gentiles through Jesus Christ, and that we might receive the promise of the Spirit through faith.

The Function of the Law

[15] Brothers, I speak as a man; though it is just a man's covenant, if it is confirmed, no man annuls or adds to it. [16] Now to Abraham and his seed were the promises made. He did not say, to "seeds", as in many; but of one, and to your seed, which is Jesus Christ. [17] Now I say this, the law, which was four hundred and thirty years later, cannot void the covenant that was confirmed by God in Christ, nor can it be invalidated that it should put an end to the promise. [18] If the inheritance is of the law, it is no longer of promise:

but God gave it to Abraham by promise.

[19] Then what purpose does the law serve? It was added because of sin, till the Seed should come to whom the promise was made; and it was administered through angels in the hand of a mediator. [20] Now a mediator does not mediate for only one, but God is one. [21] So is the law against the promises of God? God forbid: if there was a law given that could have given life, then righteousness would have been by the law. [22] But the scripture has imprisoned all under sin that the promise by faith in Jesus Christ may be given to those who believe.

[23] But before faith came, we were detained under the law, held prisoner until faith would later be revealed. [24] Therefore, the law was our guardian to bring us to Christ, that we might be justified by faith. [25] But after faith came, we are no longer under a guardian. [26] For you are all the children of God by faith in Christ Jesus. [27] For all who have been baptized into Christ have put on Christ. [28] There is neither Jew nor Greek, bond nor free, and there is neither male nor female: for you are all one in Christ Jesus. [29] And if you belong to Christ, then you are Abraham's seed, and heirs according to the promise.

CHAPTER 4

Jesus Redeemed Us from the Law

4 Let me put it this way, "The heir, as long as he is a

child, is no different than a servant, even though he is lord of all; 2 but is under tutors and administrators until the time appointed by his father." 3 Likewise, when we were children, we were enslaved to the elements of this world, 4 but when the appointed time had come, God sent out His Son, born of a woman, born under the law, 5 to redeem those who were under the law, that we might receive the adoption as sons. 6 And because you are sons, God has sent the Spirit of His Son into your hearts, crying out, "Daddy, Father." 7 For this reason you are no longer a slave, but a son; and if a son, then an heir of God through Christ.

8 But at that time, when you did not know God, you were slaves to them, which by nature, are not gods. 9 But now, after you have known God, or rather known by God, how can you turn again to the weak and poor elements, for which you desire again to be in bondage to? 10 You observe days, months, seasons and years. 11 I am frightened for you, lest I have labored for you to no avail.

Paul's Concern for the Galatians

12 Brothers, I ask you, be like me, for I am like you: for you have not done wrong by me at all. 13 You know how, through sickness in my body, I preached the gospel to you at first. 14 And the trial which you experienced because of my physical body, you did not despise or reject; but you received me as a messenger of God, even as Christ Jesus. 15 Where is the blessing you speak of? For I testify, that if it

had been possible, you would have plucked out your own eyes and would have given them to me. [16] Have I become your enemy because I tell you the truth? [17] They zealously court you, but for a purpose that is not good; yes, they want to shut you out, that you may be zealous for them. [18] It is good to always be zealous in good things, and not only when I am there with you. [19] My little children, of whom I again suffer greatly until Christ is formed in you. [20] I desire to be there with you now, and to change my tone of voice; because I am at a loss concerning you.

The Bond and Free Son

[21] Tell me, you that desire to be under the law, do you not hear the law? [22] For it is written, "Abraham had two sons, one by his slave, and the other by a woman who is free." [23] But, the child of the slave was born after the flesh, and the child of the free woman was by promise, [24] of which I speak allegorically: for these are the two covenants; the one from Mount Sinai, which bears children for slavery, which is Hagar. [25] For this Hagar is Mount Sinai in Arabia, which corresponds to Jerusalem which now is, and is in slavery with her children, [26] but the Jerusalem which is above is free, which is the mother of us all.

[27] For it is written, "Rejoice, O barren that does not bear; burst out in tears, you that do not suffer greatly: for the desolate has many more children than she who has a husband."

[28] Now brothers, we, as Isaac was, are the children of

promise.

²⁹ But, just as it was then, he which was born after the flesh, persecuted he that was born after the Spirit, so it is now.

³⁰ What does the scripture say? Cast out the slave woman and her son: for the son of the slave will not be heir with the son of the free woman.

³¹ So, brothers, we are not the children of the slave woman, but of the free.

CHAPTER 5

The Dangers of Legalism

5 Therefore, stand in the liberty which Christ has made us free, and do not be subject again to a yoke of slavery.

² Look I, Paul, am saying to you, that if you have yourselves circumcised, Christ will profit you nothing. ³ For I testify again to every man who is circumcised, that he is obligated to do the whole law. ⁴ You have become estranged from Christ and have fallen from grace, if you attempt to be justified by the law. ⁵ For we, through the Holy Spirit, by faith, wait for the hope of righteousness. ⁶ For in Christ Jesus, neither circumcision nor uncircumcision amounts to nothing, but it is by faith that works through love.

⁷ You ran well; "who stopped you from obeying the truth?"

⁸ This persuasion does not come from Him who calls you. ⁹ A little leaven leavens the whole batch of dough. ¹⁰ I have confidence regarding you in the Lord that you will not think otherwise: but he that troubles you will bear his judgment, whoever he is. ¹¹ And brothers, if I still preach circumcision, why do I still suffer persecution? Wouldn't the offense of the cross cease? ¹² How I wish those who trouble you would be cut off.

¹³ For, brothers, you have been called to have freedom; but do not use your freedom as an occasion for the flesh, but serve one another through love. ¹⁴ For the entirety of the law is fulfilled in one statement, "You shall love your neighbor as yourself." ¹⁵ But if you bite and devour one another, watch out lest you be consumed by one another.

Walk in the Spirit

¹⁶ I say then, "Walk in the Spirit, and you will not fulfill the lust of the flesh." ¹⁷ For the flesh lusts against the Spirit and the Spirit against the flesh, and these two are hostile one toward the other, so that you do not do the things you wish. ¹⁸ But if you are led by the Holy Spirit, you are not under the law. ¹⁹ Now the works of the flesh are clearly seen, which are: adultery, sexual immorality, filthiness, lewdness, ²⁰ idolatry, sorcery, contention, jealousy, rageful outburst, selfish ambitions, discord, divisions, ²¹ envy, murders, drunkenness, orgies, and the like: of which I warn you, as I have also warned you in times past, that they who do such things will not inherit the kingdom of God. ²² But

the fruit of the Holy Spirit is love, joy, peace, patience, kindness, generosity, faith, [23] humility, self-control; against such there is no law. [24] And those who belong to Christ have crucified the flesh with its passions and deep desires.

[25] If we live in the Holy Spirit, let us also follow in the footsteps of the Holy Spirit. [26] Let us not become conceited, provoking one another, having envy of one another.

CHAPTER 6

6 Brothers, if a man is caught in wrongdoing, you who are spiritual restore such a one in the spirit of gentleness; keeping watch over yourself lest you also be tempted. [2] Bear one another's burdens, doing so fulfills the law of Christ. [3] For if someone thinks himself to be something, when he is nothing, he deceives himself. [4] Let everyone examine his own work, and then he will be able to boast in himself, and not in another. [5] For every man will bear his own load.

[6] Let him who is instructed in the word share in all good things to him that teaches. [7] Do not be deceived; God is not mocked: whatever a man sows, that he will also reap. [8] For he that sows to the flesh, will of the flesh reap destruction; but he that sows to the Holy Spirit, will of the Holy Spirit reap everlasting life. [9] Let us not become discouraged while doing good, for at the appointed time

we shall reap, if we do not faint. [10] As we have opportunity, let us do good to all, especially those who are members of the faith.

[11] You see how large a letter I have written to you with my own hand. [12] As many as desire to make a good showing in the flesh, they compel you to be circumcised; this is so they will not be persecuted for the cross of Christ. [13] For not even those who are circumcised keep the law: but they desire to have you circumcised so they can boast in your flesh. [14] God forbid that I should boast, except in the cross of our Lord Jesus Christ, by whom the world has been crucified to me, and I to the world. [15] For in Christ Jesus, circumcision nor uncircumcision amounts to anything, but a new creation. [16] And for all who walk according to this rule, may peace and mercy be upon them, and upon the Israel of God.

[17] From now on let no man trouble me: for I bear the marks of the Lord Jesus Christ in my body.

[18] Brothers, the grace of our Lord Jesus Christ be with your spirit. Amen.

Unto the Galatians written from Rome.

THE EPISTLE OF PAUL THE APOSTLE

TO THE

EPHESIANS

CHAPTER 1

1 Paul, an apostle of Jesus Christ, by the will of God, to the saints who reside at Ephesus, and to the faithful in Christ Jesus, ² grace and peace to you, from God our Father, and Lord Jesus Christ.

Our Redemption in Christ

³ Blessed be the God and Father of our Lord Jesus Christ, who has blessed us with all spiritual blessings from God, in Christ, ⁴ just as He has chosen us, in Him, before the creation of the world, that we should be holy and unblemished before Him in love: ⁵ having decided beforehand that we should be adopted as sons through Jesus Christ unto Himself, according to the good pleasure of His will. ⁶ To the praise and glory of His grace, who has shown kindness to us in the Beloved. ⁷ In whom we have redemption through His blood, the forgiveness of sins, according to riches of His grace; ⁸ which He provided in abundance to us in all wisdom and understanding; ⁹ having revealed to us the mystery of His will, according to His desire which He planned beforehand in Jesus Christ. ¹⁰ For

the administration when time is complete, that He may bring together in one, everybody that is in Christ Jesus, of those who are in heaven and those who are on earth – in Him. [11] In Him, we have also obtained an inheritance, having been predestined, according to His plan, who works all things according to the counsel of His own will: [12] that we, who first placed our hope in Christ, should be for His praise and glory. [13] In Him you have trusted, after you heard the word of truth, which is the gospel of your salvation: in Him, after you believed, you were sealed with the Holy Spirit of promise. [14] Who is the down payment on our inheritance, until our purchased possession is delivered, to His praise and glory.

Paul's Prayer for Revelation and Understanding

[15] For this reason I too, having heard of your faith in the Lord Jesus, and the love you have toward all the saints, [16] do not cease to give thanks for you, making mention of you in my prayers; [17] that the God of our Lord Jesus Christ, the Father of glory, may give to you the Spirit of wisdom and revelation in the knowledge of Him: [18] Having the eyes of your understanding illuminated; that you may know what is the hope of His calling, and what the riches of the glory of His inheritance in the saints, [19] And what is the enormous greatness of His power toward us who believe, according to the working of His mighty power. [20] Which He brought about in Christ, when He raised Him from the dead, and set Him at His own right hand in His heavenly abode. [21] High above all rulers and authority,

power and dominion, and every name that is named, not only in this world, but also in the world to come: [22] And He has put all under His feet, and gave to Him to be the head over all things to the church, [23] which is His body, the fullness of Him that fills all in all.

CHAPTER 2

By His Grace Through Faith

2 And you who were dead in faults and sins; [2] whereas before, you walked according to the system of this world, according to the "Prince – Power of the Air", which is the spirit that now works in the children of disobedience. [3] Among whom we all have previously lived according to the lust of the flesh and the evil desires of the flesh and of the mind; and were by nature the children of wrath, even as others were. [4] But God, who has an abundance of mercy, because of His great love which He, loved us, [5] even when we were dead in sins, has made us alive with Christ, (by grace you are saved;) [6] and has raised us up in Him, and has caused us to sit down with Jesus Christ in heavenly places: [7] that in the ages to come, He could demonstrate the immeasurable riches of His grace, and His goodness toward us through Christ Jesus. [8] For by grace, through faith, are you saved; through nothing you have done, it is the gift of God: [9] Not by our works, lest any should boast. [10] For we are His creation, created in Christ Jesus for good works, which God has ordained beforehand, that we should walk in them.

Brought Near By The Blood Of Jesus

[11] Therefore remember, in times past, being Gentiles in the flesh, you were called "Uncircumcision" by those who are called "Circumcision" in the flesh, which is made by hands; [12] that at that time you did not know Christ, being foreigners with no citizenship in Israel, and strangers to the covenants of promise, without hope, and without God in this world: [13] But now in Christ Jesus, you who were far away are now made near by the blood of Christ.

Jesus Unifies Jew And Gentile

[14] For He is our peace, who has made both "Jew and Gentile" one, and has broken down the hedge between us. [15] Having, in His flesh, abolished the hatred of the law of commandments that are contained in the ordinances; to create in Himself, out of the two, one new man, therefore making peace; [16] so that He could reconcile both to God in one body "through the cross", thereby killing the hostility: [17] And He came and preached peace to you who were far away, and to those who were close by. [18] For through Him we both, "Jew and Gentile", have access by one Spirit to the Father.

Jesus Is Our Chief Cornerstone

[19] Therefore you are no longer strangers and foreigners, but fellow citizens with the saints, and members of the household of God, [20] and are built upon the foundation

of the apostles and prophets, Jesus Christ Himself being the chief cornerstone; [21] In whom the building is joined together and grows into a holy temple in the Lord. [22] In whom you are also built up together for a dwelling place of God through the Spirit.

CHAPTER 3

The Mystery Of Christ Revealed

3 For this reason, I Paul, the prisoner of Jesus Christ for you Gentiles, [2] having heard of the dispensation of the grace of God which is given from me to you: [3] How by revelation He made known to me the mystery; as I wrote before in a few words, [4] which when you read, you will be able to understand my knowledge concerning the mystery of Christ. [5] Which in past generations was not revealed to the sons of men, as it is now revealed to His holy apostles and prophets by the Spirit; [6] That the Gentiles should be co-heirs, of the same body, and partakers of His promise in Christ through the gospel: [7] Of which I became a servant, according to the gift of God's grace given to me by the effective working of His power.

God's Purpose For This Mystery

[8] To me, who is the very least of all saints, is this grace given, that I should preach among the Gentiles the fathomless riches of Christ; [9] to make all men see what the

fellowship of the mystery is, which from the beginning of the world was hid in God, who created all by Jesus Christ: [10] in order that the manifold wisdom of God might be made known through the church to the principalities and powers in heavenly places, [11] according to the eternal plan which He performed through Christ Jesus our Lord: [12] In whom we have courage and access with confidence through faith in Him.

[13] Therefore, I desire that you do not be discouraged over my afflictions for you, which is your glory. [14] For this reason I bow my knees to the Father of our Lord Jesus Christ, [15] of whom the entire family in heaven and earth is named, [16] that He would give you, according to the riches of His glory, to be strong with the power of His Spirit in the inner man; [17] that Christ may inhabit your hearts through faith, that you may be rooted and grounded in love. [18] That you are able to understand with all saints, the width, and length, and depth, and height; [19] and to know the love of Christ, which goes beyond all knowledge, that you be filled with the fullness of God.

[20] Now to Him that is able to do far more than we could ever ask or think, according to the power that works inside of us. [21] To Him be the glory in the church by Christ Jesus throughout all generations for all eternity. Amen.

CHAPTER 4

Encouraged to Walk in Unity

4 Therefore, I, the prisoner of the Lord, earnestly ask that you walk worthy of the calling, with which you were called, ² with all humility and gentleness, with patience, accepting one another in love; ³ doing your best to keep the unity of the Spirit in the bond of peace. ⁴ There is one body and one Spirit, even as you were called in one hope of your calling; ⁵ one Lord, one faith, one baptism, ⁶ one God and Father of all, who is above all, and through all, and in you all.

Spiritual Gifts Given to Man

⁷ But to each one of us is given grace according to measure of Christ's gift. ⁸ Therefore He said, when He ascended on high, he led captivity captive, and gave gifts to men. ⁹ Now that He ascended, "what does it mean except that He also descended into the lower regions of the earth?" ¹⁰ He that descended is also the same one who ascended far above all heavens, that He might fulfill all things.

¹¹ And He gave to some, apostles; and to some prophets; and to some evangelists; and to some, shepherds and teachers. ¹² For the equipping of the saints, for the work of ministry, and for building up the body of Christ: ¹³ till we all come to the unity of the faith, and to the knowledge of the Son of God, to a complete man, to the measure of maturity of the fullness of Christ: ¹⁴ that we no longer be children, tossed around and carried about with every wind of doctrine, by the trickery of men, and cunning craftiness,

whereby they lie in wait to deceive; [15] But speaking the truth in love, that we may in all things grow up into Him: Christ, who is the head, [16] from whom the whole body is fitly joined and held together by that which every joint supplies, according to the effective work in the measure of every part, making the body grow unto the edifying of itself in love.

The Old and New Man

[17] Therefore, this I say and testify in the Lord, that you no longer walk as other Gentiles walk, in the futility of their mind, [18] having their understanding darkened, being alienated from the life of God through the ignorance that is in them, because of their blindness of heart: [19] who having become calloused have given themselves up to sensuality, to practice all sorts of immorality with greediness.

[20] But this is not how you learned Christ. [21] If you have heard Him, and have been taught by Him, as the truth is in Jesus: [22] then lay aside the former behavior of the old man, which is morally corrupt through deceitful desires; [23] be renewed in the spirit of your mind. [24] And put on the new man, which is created after God in righteousness and true holiness.

Watching Our Words – Grieving the Holy Spirit

[25] Therefore, put away lying, and let every man speak truth to his neighbor: for we are members of one another. [26] Be angry and do not sin: do not let the sun set on your anger.

[27] Do not give occasion to the devil. [28] Let the one who is stealing steal no more: but let him grow weary working with his own hands that which is good, that he may give to the needs of others. [29] Do not let bad words come out your mouth, but that which is good for the use of edifying, that it may minister grace to those who hear. [30] Do not grieve the Holy Spirit of God, by which you are sealed for the "day of redemption". [31] Let all bitterness, and indignation, and wrath, and clamor, and evil speaking be removed from you, along with evil intentions. [32] And be kind to one another, tenderhearted, forgiving each other just as God in Christ forgave you.

CHAPTER 5

Walk In Love

5 Therefore, be imitators of God, as beloved children; [2]

and walk in love, even as Christ loved us, and gave Himself for us, an offering and a sacrifice to God for a sweet smelling odor.

[3] Do not let fornication, uncleanness or covetousness be named among you, as is becoming to saints; [4] nor let filthiness, nor foolish or dirty talking which are not fitting, but rather let there be thanksgiving. [5] For you know that every fornicator, or unclean person, or covetous man, or anyone who worships idols, will not have an inheritance in the kingdom of the Messiah and of God.

Walk As Children of Light – Not Darkness

[6] Let no one deceive you with empty words; it is on account of these things that the wrath of God comes upon the sons of disobedience. [7] Therefore, do not be partakers with them. [8] For you were once darkness, but now light in the Lord; so walk as children of light. [9] (For the fruit of the Spirit is in all goodness, righteousness, and truth). [10] Proving what is well pleasing to the Lord; [11] and do not have fellowship with the unfruitful works of darkness, but rather expose them. [12] For the things being done by them in secret is shameful to even talk about. [13] But all things that are exposed by the light is revealed: for everything that is made known is light.

[14] Therefore He says, "Awake you who sleep, and rise up from the dead, and the Messiah will shine upon you."

Walk as the Wise

[15] Therefore, pay attention to how accurately you walk, not as the unwise, but as the wise, [16] making good use of time, because the days are evil. [17] On this account do not be foolish, but understanding what the will of the Lord is. [18] Do not get drunk on wine; in which is debauchery , but be filled with the Spirit. [19] Speaking to each other in psalms and hymns and spiritual songs, singing and praising in your heart to the Lord; [20] giving thanks at all times, for all things, in the name of our Lord Jesus Christ to Him who is God and the Father. [21] Being subject to one another out of reverence for God.

Instructions for Husbands and Wives

[22] Wives, submit yourself to your husband, as you do to the Lord. [23] For the husband is the superior of the wife, even as Christ is the superior of the church; and He is the Savior of the body. [24] Even as the church is subject to Christ, let the wife also be subject to her husband in everything.

[25] Husbands, love your wives in the same way Christ loved the church, and gave Himself for her. [26] That He might make her holy and cleanse her by the washing of water by the word. [27] That He might present to Himself a glorious church, not having spot or wrinkle or any such things; but that it might be holy and blameless. [28] So men should love their wives like their own body. He that loves his wife loves himself. [29] For no one, at any time, has hated his own flesh, but nourishes and cherishes it, just as the Lord does the church. [30] For we are members of His flesh, of His body, and of His bones. [31] Because of this shall a man leave his father and mother and be joined to his wife, and the two shall be one flesh. [32] This mystery is great, but I speak concerning Christ and to the church. [33] However, let everyone of you love his wife as he does himself, and the wife that she may reverence her husband.

CHAPTER 6

Instructions for Children and Parents

6 Children, obey your parents in the Lord, for this is the right thing to do. ² Honor your Father and Mother; (which is the first commandment with a promise;) ³ that it may go well for you, and that you may live a long life on earth. ⁴ Fathers, do not provoke your children, but bring them up in the discipline and admonition of the Lord.

Instructions for Slaves and Masters

⁵ Slaves , obey your masters according to the flesh with fear and trembling, in simplicity of heart, as you would do for Christ. ⁶ Not just to be seen or impress others; but as slaves of the Messiah, doing the will of God from your soul, ⁷ with good will, as being a slave to the Lord and not to man: ⁸ Knowing that whatever good any man does, he shall receive the same from the Lord, whether he is a slave or a free person.

⁹ And masters, do the same to them, give up threats, knowing that your own Master is in heaven, and there is no respect of persons with Him.

Spiritual Wickedness in Heavenly Places

¹⁰ Finally brothers, be strong in the Lord, and the power of His might. ¹¹ Put on the full armor of God, so you will be able to stand against the craftiness of the devil: ¹² because we do not wrestle against flesh and blood, but against principalities, against the world's-ruler of darkness of this age, and against the spiritual powers of wickedness in heavenly places. ¹³ because of this put on the full armor of God that you may be able to hold your ground in the Day

of Evil; and having overcome all things to stand. [14] Stand therefore, having the truth wrapped around your loins, and having on the chest piece of righteousness; [15] and having shod your feet with the readiness of the gospel of peace: [16] Above all, taking the shield of faith, with which you will be able to extinguish all the fiery darts of the Evil One. [17] And take hold of the helmet of salvation, and the sword of the Spirit, which is the word of God:

[18] praying in the Spirit always with prayer and supplication, remaining watchful with all perseverance and prayer for all the saints. [19] And for me, that the word may be given that I speak boldly to reveal the mystery of the gospel, [20] for which I am an ambassador in chains: that in this I may speak boldly, as I should speak.

Paul Sends Tychicus

[21] But that you may also know the things concerning me and how I am doing, Tychicus, a dear brother and faithful minister in the Lord, will make known to you all things. [22] Whom I sent to you for this very purpose, that you may know our affairs, and that he might comfort your hearts.

[23] Peace to the brethren, and love with faith, from God the Father and our Lord Jesus Christ.

Written from Rome to the Ephesians by Tychicus.

THE FIRST EPISTLE OF PAUL THE APOSTLE

TO THE

PHILIPPIANS

CHAPTER 1

1 Paul and Timothy, the slaves of Jesus Christ, to all those set apart by God in Christ Jesus, which are at Philippi, with the overseers and deacons: [2] grace to you and peace from God our Father, and from the Lord Jesus Christ.

Paul Expresses His Thankfulness

[3] I thank my God on every remembrance of you, [4] always in every prayer of mine for you all, making my prayer with joy, [5] for your fellowship in the good news of Jesus from the first day until now; [6] convinced of this very thing, that He which has begun a good work in you will finish it until the day of Jesus Christ: [7] just as it is right for me to think this of you all, because I hold you in my heart; inasmuch as both in my chains, and in the defense and validation of the gospel, you are all partakers of grace with me. [8] For God is my witness, how I long for you all with the love of Jesus Christ. [9] And this is my prayer; that your love may abound yet all the more in knowledge and all discernment; [10] that you may judge as good those things that are excellent; that

you may be pure and blameless till the day of Christ; [11] being filled with the fruits of righteousness, which is through Jesus Christ, to the glory and praise of God.

Paul's Boldness While in Prison

[12] It is my desire that you know, brothers, that the things which happened to me came about to further the gospel; [13] so that my chains in Christ are visible to all the palace guard, and all other places also; [14] and many of the brothers in the Lord, persuaded by my chains, are even more bold to speak the word without fear.

[15] Some indeed preach Christ out of jealousy and strife; and some out of good will: [16] one preaches Christ out of selfish ambition, not out of sincerity, thinking to add affliction to my chains. [17] But others out of love, knowing that I am appointed for the defense of the gospel.

Gospel Preached through False Motive

[18] By all means, notwithstanding, that in every way, whether by false motive, or in truth, Christ is preached; and I in this do rejoice, yes, and will rejoice. [19] For I know that this will turn to my deliverance through your prayers, and the assistance of the Spirit of Jesus Christ, [20] according to my eager expectation and my hope, that in not one thing shall I be ashamed, but, as always, with all boldness shall Christ be magnified in my body, whether it be by life or death.

To live is Christ – To Die is Gain

[21] For to me, to live is Christ, and to die is gain. [22] But if I continue living in the flesh, this means more fruit for my labor: yet which to choose I do not know. [23] For I am hard pressed between the two, having a desire to leave and to be with Christ; which is far better: [24] nevertheless, to remain in the flesh is more necessary for you. [25] And having this confidence, I know that I will remain and continue with all of you for the furtherance of your joy in the faith; [26] that your rejoicing may abound in Jesus Christ for me, by my coming to you again.

[27] Conduct your life in a manner worthy of the gospel of Christ: that whether I come to see you or go away, that I may hear that you continue to stand in one spirit, with one mind, working for the faith of the gospel; [28] do not be frightened by your adversaries: which to them is proof of destruction, but to you deliverance, and that from God. [29] For to you it is given on behalf of Christ, to not only believe in Him, but to also suffer for His sake; [30] having the same struggle that you saw in me, and now hear is in me.

CHAPTER 2

Jesus – The Perfect Example of Humility

2 Therefore, if there be any encouragement in Christ, any comfort of love, any fellowship of the Spirit, if any affection or mercy, [2] to complete my joy, that you think alike, having the same love, being harmonious, of one mind. [3] Let nothing be done through selfishness and conceit; but in humility let each esteem the other better than himself. [4] Let not every man look out for his own interest, but also for the interest of others. [5] Let this way of thinking be in you, which was also in Christ Jesus. [6] Who, being in the form of God, did not think it robbery to be equal with God, [7] but emptied himself and took upon himself the form of a slave, and was made in the likeness of men: [8] and being in the form of man, He humbled Himself and became obedient to death, even the death of the cross. [9] Therefore, God has highly exalted Jesus, and given Him a name which is above every name: [10] that at the name of Jesus every knee will bow, of those who are in heaven, and of those who are on earth, and of those under the earth; [11] and every tongue will confess that Jesus Christ is Lord, to the glory of God the Father.

[12] Therefore, my beloved, as you have always obeyed, not just in my presence only, but even more in my absence; with fear and trembling, achieve your own salvation. [13] For it is God which works in you, that you desire to do His good will.

[14] Do all things without griping and arguing. [15] That you may be blameless and pure, the sons of God, unblemished, in the middle of a dishonest and perverse nation, among whom you shine as lights in the world. [16] Holding firmly to the word of life; that I may rejoice in the day of Christ, knowing that I have not run or labored in vain. [17] Yes, and if I am to be offered up as the sacrifice and minister of your

faith, I will have joy and rejoice with you all. [18] For the same reason you also have joy, and rejoice with me.

Timothy and Epaphroditus

[19] But I trust in the Lord Jesus to send Timothy to you shortly, that I also may be encouraged when I know your condition. [20] For I have no one like-minded who will genuinely be concerned for you. [21] For all seek their own interest, not the things of Jesus Christ. [22] But you know his character, that as a son with the father, he has served with me in the gospel. [23] Therefore I hope to send him at once, as soon as I see how it will go with me. [24] But I also am convinced in the Lord that I too shall come shortly. [25] Yet I thought it necessary to send to you Epaphroditus, my brother, and fellow laborer, and fellow soldier, but your messenger, and he that ministered to my needs. [26] For he longed for you all, and was troubled, because you had heard that he had been ill. [27] For he indeed was sick, almost near death, but God had mercy on him; and not him only, but me also, lest I should have been overcome with grief. [28] Therefore I have sent him with haste, that when you see him again, you may rejoice, and that I may be free from anxiety. [29] Therefore, receive him in the Lord with all joy; and hold such men in high esteem; [30] because for the work of Christ he was near death, not regarding his own life, in order to supply your shortcoming of service toward me.

CHAPTER 3

Paul's Example

3 Finally, my brothers, rejoice in the Lord. To write the same things over to you is not bothersome to me, but it is safe for you.

[2] Beware of dogs, beware of evil workers, beware of those who force circumcision on believers. [3] For we are the circumcision, who worship God in the Spirit, and rejoice in Christ Jesus, and put no trust in the flesh. [4] Though I might also trust in the flesh, if any other man thinks he has reason to trust in the flesh, I more so, [5] being circumcised on the eighth day, of the family of Israel, of the tribe of Benjamin, a Hebrew of the Hebrews, and concerning the law, a Pharisee,

[6] concerning zeal, I persecuted the church, concerning the righteousness which is in the law, I was blameless.

[7] But what were gain for me, those I have counted loss for Christ. [8] Indeed, I count all things as a loss for the surpassing greatness of knowing Christ Jesus my Lord; for whom I have suffered the loss of all, and count them as garbage, that I may win Christ, [9] and be found in Him, not having my own righteousness, which is through the law, but that which is through the faith of Christ, the righteousness from God by faith: [10] that I may know Him,

and the power of His resurrection, and that I may share in His sufferings, being made like Him in His death; [11] if, in some way, I may attain the resurrection from the dead.

Forget the Things Behind – Reach Out For the Things Ahead

[12] Not as though I have already obtained, or have already been perfected: but I press on that I may seize that for which Christ Jesus has also laid hold of me. [13] Brothers, I do not consider myself as having apprehended: but there is one thing I do, forgetting what lies behind me, and reaching out for the things which lie ahead, [14] I run straight toward the goal to win the prize of the upward calling of God in Christ Jesus. [15] Therefore, all that are mature in Christ, let us have this mind: and if in anything you think differently, God will reveal even this to you. [16] In any case, to the extent we have already attained, let us hold to the same principles, and let us be of the same mind.

[17] Brothers, be fellow imitators of me, and observe those who walk this way, as you have us for an example. [18] For many walk, of whom I have told you about many times, and weeping now as I tell you, that they are the enemies of the cross of Christ, [19] whose destiny is eternal destruction, whose God is their own appetite, whose glory is in their shame, whose mind is on earthly things. [20] For our citizenship is in heaven; from where we also look for the Savior, the Lord Jesus Christ, [21] who will transform our weak mortal body, that it may be like His

glorious body, according to the power whereby He is able to subdue all things unto Himself.

CHAPTER 4

4 Therefore, my brothers, whom I love and long for, my joy and crown, continue to stand in the Lord, my beloved.

2 I encourage Euodias and I encourage Syntyche that they be in agreement in the Lord. 3 And I ask you also, my true partner, help those who labored with me in the gospel, with Clement also, and with my other fellow laborers whose names are in the book of life.

Rejoice in the Lord at All Times

4 Be joyful in the Lord at all times, again I say, be joyful. 5 Let your gentle spirit be known to all men. The coming of the Lord is near. 6 Be anxious for nothing; but in every situation by prayer and petition, with thanksgiving, let your requests be made known to God. 7 And the peace of God, which is beyond comprehension, will keep your hearts and minds through Christ Jesus.

8 Finally brothers, whatever is true, whatever is honest, whatever is just, whatever is pure, whatever is pleasing, whatever is of a good report; if there be any excellence of character, if there be any praise, let your thoughts dwell on these things. 9 Those things which you have learned and received, and heard, and seen in me, do those things: and

the God of peace will be with you.

In Whatever State Be Content

[10] I have great joy in the Lord, that now at last your thoughtful concern for me has flourished again; though you were concerned for my welfare, you lacked the opportunity. [11] Not that I speak in regard to being in need: for I have learned, in whatever state I am in, to be content. [12] I know how to be brought low by poverty, and I know how to live in abundance: everywhere and in all things I have learned to both be full and to be hungry, both of having abundance and suffering need. [13] I can do all things through Christ who gives me strength. [14] In any case, you have done well, that you became partners with me in my time of trouble.

[15] Now you Philippians know, that in the beginning of the gospel, when I left Macedonia, no church shared with me concerning giving and receiving, but you only. [16] For even in Thessalonica, on more than one occasion, you sent gifts for my needs. [17] Not that I seek a gift: but I do seek the abundant harvest to your account. [18] I have been paid in full and have abundance: I have all I need, having received your gifts sent by Epaphroditus, a fragrant smelling and acceptable sacrifice that is well pleasing to God. [19] And my God will fully provide your every need according to His riches in glory by Christ Jesus. [20] Now to God our Father be glory for ever and ever. Amen.

Conclusion

21 Greet every saint in Christ Jesus. The brothers that are with me greet you. 22 All the saints greet you, especially those that are of Caesar's family.

23 The grace of our Lord Jesus Christ be with you all. Amen.

Written to the Philippians from Rome by Epaphroditus.

You can read more online and follow the development of the TRIB Bible by visiting us @ tribnewtestament.com.

If you find any errors you would like to report or send me a comment about this book or the TRIB Bible, you can do so by e-mailing davidbroom@tribnewtestament.com or by snail mail to:

David Broom Ministries
1412 14th Circle
Barling, AR 72923

www.ingramcontent.com/pod-product-compliance
Lightning Source LLC
Chambersburg PA
CBHW060507030426
42337CB00015B/1787